PRAISE FOR

"*Hard Bargain* is a beautifully [...] to Donald Denihan's unwavering faith in God. He takes great care to provide an objective prospective on how he handled three gripping 'Life Events' that challenged his resilience in mind, body, and spirit. The book takes the reader on an emotional rollercoaster ride through Denihan's honest narration of three true stories of tremendous courage, stamina, and survival."

—*Paul L. Cuneo, Managing Director of Wealth Management at UBS Financial Services*

"I couldn't put *Hard Bargain* down, once I started it. Donald Denihan's courage to share his personal story is a testament to his inner strength and resilience. The depth of his journey, the enormous struggles and health challenges he bravely faced, are not only moving, but also deeply inspiring. His book is not just a series of beautifully woven stories; it's a powerful reminder of the human spirit and the importance of faith." —*Rose Lavelle, Professor of Management & Finance at Molloy University*

"Donald Denihan chronicles his three close brushes with death and delves into these experiences in a unique and heartfelt way. His book allows us to see how he turned potentially terrible circumstances into positive, relationship-building events. His thoughts, words and feelings make us contemplate our own relationships with those we encounter peripherally and those whom we hold nearest and dearest. An unforgettable read."

—*John A Procaccino, MD Chief, Division of Colon and Rectal Surgery, NSUH Manhasset*

"In *Hard Bargain*, Donald Denihan has captured just about every human element there is: loneliness, anxiety, depression, hope, despair, jubilation, determination and inner peace. his voice is very clear to the point I felt he was speaking only to me. Donald is an inspiration to all and a great example of what it is to be a friend and a true husband and father."

—Jorge Pelaez, Chief Capital Officer, 3 Rivers Energy Partners

"I loved *Hard Bargain.* It reminded me of the ultimate 'adrift at sea' story is Nathaniel Philbrick's *In the Heart of the Sea*, which was also based on the true story. Thankfully, things ended better for Donald and we are fortunate for the opportunity that gave him to write this book."   *—Robert Benjamin, partner at Wiggin and Dana LLP*

"*Hard Bargain* is a vivid and clear-eyed view into the formative life stories of Donald Denihan Throughout the book, we see a man faced with some serious challenges – any one of which could lead someone to say, 'why me,' resentfully blaming oneself and the world around them for youthful mistakes, health scares, and a real version of 'Gilligan's Island' where a day of fishing turns into a life and death struggle. The matter-of-factness of the storytelling puts the reader right into the experiences, inviting our own questions of 'who am I, who might I be if put to life endangering tests?' *Hard Bargain* is an engaging and, if so inclined, a 'make-you-think' book—well done!"

—Nancy Drozdow, Founder and Principal, CFAR, Inc.

"This book brought out the multitude of emotions Donald Denihan experienced as he confronted death so many times. You can literally feel the fear, hope, disappointment, grit, and. You empathize for what he went through and are relieved that this wonderful person is still here to share his experiences with us. I am so proud of what he has written and it has made me more thankful for every day. You are truly missing out if you do not read this book. I will cherish it forever."

—Tom Zanecchia, Founder and President of
Wealth Management Consultants

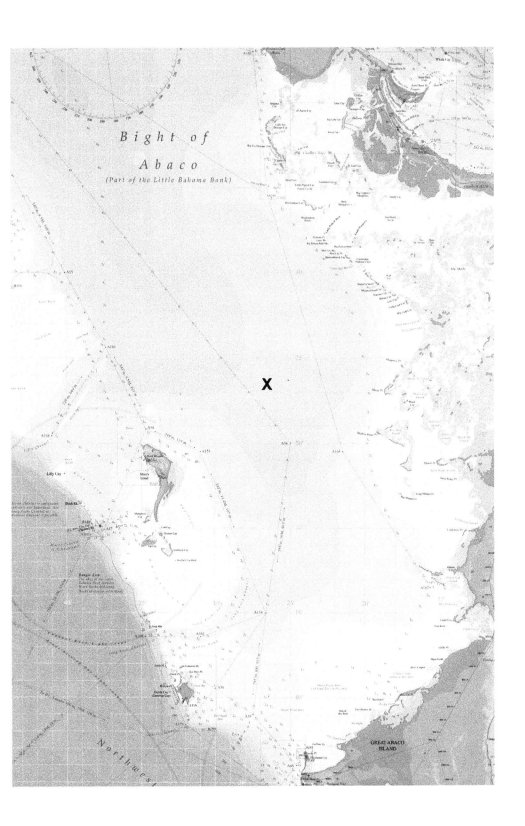

HARD BARGAIN

WHAT LIFE-ALTERING EXPERIENCES TAUGHT ME ABOUT FAITH, FRIENDSHIP, AND FAMILY

DONALD G. DENIHAN

with JON LAND

Names: Denihan, Donald G., author. | Land, Jon, author.
Title: Hard bargain : what life-altering experiences taught me about faith, friendship, and family / Donald G. Denihan, with Jon Land.
Description: First Stillwater River Publications edition. | West Warwick, RI, USA : Stillwater River Publications, [2024]
Identifiers: ISBN: 978-1-963296-35-8 (paperback) | LCCN: 2024906033
Subjects: LCSH: Denihan, Donald G. | Near-death experiences. | Hunting accidents. | Cancer—Patients—Biography. | Fishing accidents. | Survival. | Faith. | LCGFT: Autobiographies.
Classification: LCC: BF1045.N4 D46 2024 | DDC: 133.9013—dc23

Survival is triumph enough.

—*Harry Crews*

For my family.

TABLE OF CONTENTS

PROLOGUE

The Storm, 2012

My index finger curled through the bow hook was all that was keeping me from slipping under the sea. The ocean currents, stirred up by the storm that showed no signs of abating, crested over my head. I held my breath, waited for the wave to pass, then sucked in some air. My eyes stung from the salt I'd been tasting and smelling for hours now.

"Please, God," our burly Bahamian guide, Alfred, kept praying. "Please God, please God, please God . . ."

Alfred was a Seventh-day Adventist, but his prayers were powerless against the storm raging around us.

"What the fuck?" my friend Gene screamed over him. "Where are the fucking people who are supposed to rescue us?"

I could see Alfred's nostrils flare in the sliver of moonlight that peeked through the storm clouds. "What you doing, mon? I'm talking to the spirit here, trying to save us! What's the matter with *yous*? You can't be talking like a—"

A gush of water slammed into Alfred's face, cutting off his words as he retched and coughed it from his mouth. He was trying to get God to help us, until Gene brought the devil onto our capsized skiff, where we were clinging for dear life.

"Shut the fuck up, Gene!" I yelled at my friend. "Shut the fuck up! Let him pray. It's the only chance we've got!"

But even Alfred's prayers couldn't change another grim reality we were facing:

Gene couldn't swim.

We'd been in the water for hours by then, around ten, I think. The storm had sprung up out of nowhere, when light still hung in a sky that turned angry with coal-black clouds. One moment it was sunny and in the next, torrents of rain belched from the sky. At least that's what it seemed like. It was easier to avoid panic in the light, but as soon as the night took hold, our world shrank to little more than the capsized boat's smooth bottom and that bow hook through which the three of us had threaded our fingers.

I thought about my wife and four children, and was filled with a fear I'd never see them again that set my heart racing. My son Patrick was fourteen, my daughter Devon was seventeen, Tim nineteen, and Donald, who had accompanied me on the trip but hadn't joined us on the boat, was twenty-one. He had stayed behind at the lodge, the best hope we had for a rescue because I knew he'd call the Bahamian Coast Guard when we failed to return to port as scheduled. Hours into our plight I heard something like the heavy *wop-wop-wop* of a helicopter, but the sound faded quickly in the storm's pounding.

The three-foot swells had us desperately struggling to bail out the accumulating water from our sixteen-foot skiff, with Tupperware containers that had held our sandwiches. The swells were the equivalent of twenty feet to a larger fishing boat, something like the kind of cabin cruiser we could only wish we'd chartered instead of a tiny flats boat. We'd run out of gas an hour into the storm, and I looked toward Alfred.

"Hey, we need to switch out the tanks."

He slid across the small deck of the skiff and lifted the second fuel container to rig it into the engine. His face went blank.

"It's empty, mon," he said meekly. "I forgot to fill it."

Our original intention was just to round the bend from the lodge, where we were staying on Abaco Island, to cast our lines there. We planned to stay out only for a few hours, but with no fish biting, Alfred offered a solution.

"I know a place, mon, I know a place where we can catch some bonefish. And dese be elephant bonefish, mon!"

Gene and I had looked at each other and thought, *Why not?* I had no idea Alfred was talking about a spot nearly thirty miles offshore, and by the time I realized it, we'd cut the engine to slow to a drift and I figured we might as well see if these elephant bonefish were biting. Alfred took his place atop a perch-like platform built over the engine and began poling for bonefish from five feet in the air.

As soon as the storm began to rage, we reached into the bow lazaret for the life jackets but found only an undersized one that Gene managed to loop a single arm through. I donned one of those yellow blow-up, airline-like versions, while Alfred ended up with a seat cushion flotation device. By the time the pounding of the larger swells ultimately capsized us, we'd lost all three to the churning sea and watched them drift away, helpless to retrieve the meager protection they provided. Our only saving grace was the mid-seventies temperature of the Bahamian waters.

We had set out from Bay Lodge on Abaco Island that morning. The lodge had been reduced to rubble by Hurricane Noel three years earlier but had been rebuilt from scratch with direct access to the Marls of Abaco, a natural system of unpressured flats that boast the best bonefishing in the world. It was far less crowded and tourist-dominated than the side of the island facing the mainland, an oasis of a destination known only to serious fly fishermen happy to cast their lines in crystal-clear waters without the frills, accounting for why I'd chosen it. The lodge maintained a regular complement of charter guides, allocating two fishermen per skiff, but the size of our party meant we needed an extra guide, so Alfred was called in to sub. As such, his sixteen-foot skiff wasn't subjected to regular inspections to make sure basic safety protocols were adhered to. Alfred had spent his life on the water and boasted that, in a similar emergency, he'd once swum fourteen miles "with my daddy on my back." By all accounts, though, we were far more than fourteen miles from any shore.

Occasionally, the rain would stop and the clouds would break, letting the light of the full moon shine down. We'd think we had finally outlasted the storm, only to have the sky darken and open up on us anew, the driving rain feeling like needles pricking our face. I fell asleep a few times, and once, when I woke up, I saw Gene had let go of the bow hook and was drifting away.

I swam after him, straying farther and farther away from the skiff. "Gene!" I screamed. "Gene!"

He was flailing in the currents when I got to him and gasping for air. I managed to get a hold of Gene and turned around to drag him back to the boat amid the dark rain splatter.

But it was gone.

PART ONE

FOOTPRINTS

One night a man had a dream. He dreamed
he was walking along the beach with the LORD.
Across the sky flashed scenes from his life.
For each scene he noticed two sets of
footprints in the sand: one belonging
to him, and the other to the LORD.

When the last scene of his life flashed before him,
he looked back at the footprints in the sand.
He noticed that many times along the path of his life,
there was only one set of footprints.
He also noticed that it happened
at the very lowest and saddest times in his life.
This really bothered him
and he questioned the LORD about it:
"LORD, you said that once I decided to follow you,
you'd walk with me all the way.
But I have noticed that during the most troublesome times
in my life, there is only one set of footprints.
I don't understand why when I needed you most
you would leave me."

The LORD replied:
"My son, my precious child,
I love you and I would never leave you.
During your times of trial and suffering,
when you see only one set of footprints,
it was when I carried you."

—Author unknown

1

THE BLIND

The night of the storm at sea wasn't the first time I had almost died.

The first came on December 29, 1977, four days after Christmas. My younger brother Laurence and I were on school vacation, so we had a lot of free time on our hands. Looking at us, you might not guess we were brothers. Laurence was blond and blue-eyed, while I had brown hair, straight like Laurence's, and blue eyes. We were both lanky in build, neither of us possessing much bulk. Still, I could manhandle him pretty easily while, as the years went on, he grew beefier and the reverse became true.

We'd enjoyed a white Christmas, and the weather had stayed windy and stormy, conditions perfect for duck hunting, and we decided once the weather broke we were going to head out onto the bay for a morning hunt. We packed our decoys and laid out our jackets, gloves, wool socks and sweaters, and my green rubber boots with yellow laces before we went to bed, to get a jump on things in the morning.

I was so cranked up that I woke at five-thirty, before my alarm even rang. Outside, it was cold, raw, and cloudy. The northern wind brought clouds and a light, variable wind as well as an unbelievably bitter chill. The water looked dismal and gray from my window, but duck hunters didn't care about that. Soon I'd be inundated by the smell of a salty marsh, the morning sky filled with magnificent colors of purple and blue...

And ducks, ours for the taking.

It was eerily quiet when I padded downstairs. My father had already gone back to work to catch up after taking a few days off, and my mother and sisters were still asleep. I had a sweet little Franchi twelve-gauge semiautomatic shotgun that was given to me as a gift by my older sister's husband, who'd fought in Vietnam. That shotgun was my pride and joy, and I practiced with it whenever I had the opportunity. Like most semiautomatics, the Franchi held five rounds in the magazine. It was only legal to load three shells, so I added a plug to remove the extra space. The gun fit me perfectly, meaning it gave me the ability to hit anything I shot at. I really liked the fact that it automatically loaded a shell after I fired, because as a new shooter that allowed me to focus on the birds.

When he got up, Laurence wasn't keen on heading out to the water in the cold, gray morning, but I was the older brother and didn't leave him much choice. We grabbed a bag of decoys, my shotgun, a pocketful of shells, our winter jackets, and gloves. Then we walked down to the water's edge, lifted the dinghy off the concrete platform on which it rested, and dragged the boat into the water. Laurence had lugged the nine-horsepower outboard engine down the thirty-five steep steps that led from the rear of our property on the bluff to the shoreline where our fourteen-foot aluminum Grumman dinghy was perched on a concrete deck, while I loaded the boat with all our gear. We made sure the outboard was firmly attached to the transom by cranking down on the clamps and connected the gas tank. We pulled the dinghy into the water, tilted down the motor so the propeller and lower unit dipped below the surface, and primed the ball. It took a few pulls to get her started, but soon enough there was water spitting out of the hose, so we climbed aboard and motored out to the blind.

The crackle of the ice around us on the water's surface sounded the whole quarter mile to where our duck blind was affixed to the bottom of the bay by a 150-pound mushroom anchor. Laurence and I had built it ourselves, after we found an old dock float that had washed up on shore. We used that as the blind's deck and constructed the walls with a combination of fresh plywood and wood debris salvaged from the shore. It took quite an effort, given that the blind had to be tall enough to stand in, with a hole cut out of the rear to climb inside and a wooden platform about the height of a serving bar making up the front. Then for camouflage we painted it military-ship gray with black spots to match the dreary bleakness of the typical morning. That was the time the ducks were most active for wide-eyed boys like me and my brother.

My father was in the dry-cleaning business, for which the soap was stored in fifty-five-gallon drums. Laurence and I had lugged a bunch of them down to the shoreline one at a time to create the platform on which the blind floated. We built it on shore and then towed it with our dinghy out into the bay.

The previous few days had been cold, and the bay was covered over with a slush of ice that hugged the water's edge. The slush was so thick that if I took the engine out of gear it would bring the skiff to a standstill, but not thick enough to keep us from reaching the blind. We were the only boat on the water, and all I heard was the slop and chop of the hull cutting through the ice and the slap of water against the aluminum hull. I figured that Cow's Bay would be loaded with ducks and the hunting would be fast, furious, and exhilarating, like Christmas come a second time.

The blind was only a quarter-mile from shore. But with the current, the wind, and the boat loaded to the gills, it took us a while to reach it. Winter on the bay was a unique time of year. A distinct salty smell hung in the air, and the high humidity left our exposed skin feeling dank and clammy. I felt cold and hot at the same time: cold from the stinging wind that seemed to freeze the sweat caked to my face and warm from the exertion of lugging all the equipment and then setting a few strings of scaup decoys on the edge of the current seam into the wind. When we were done, we headed back toward the blind to await the ducks. The tide was moving, and it wouldn't be long before they were flying . . . or so we hoped.

We maneuvered the dinghy up to the blind, tied it down to a cleat bolted into the wooden surface of the structure, and climbed in. The blind rocked but settled steady after a few moments. I leaned my shotgun in the left front corner of the blind, set up our buckets, and sat down. Every now and then we'd stand up and peek out to see if there were any ducks cruising in above the water.

Nothing.

Something wasn't right that morning, and we'd go from sitting to looking, then back to sitting, and then more looking, hoping all the while that when we looked we'd see a big flurry of ducks heading our way. But it was to no avail.

Some rain would have made for better hunting conditions, but overall, we had a pretty good day. We waited and waited and waited, while the temperature dropped and dropped. Our faces stung with cold, our hands and fingers stiffened inside our gloves.

Duck blinds were special places, comfortable enough to make you relax and primitive enough to keep you on edge. At sixteen years old, I did my best thinking in a blind, free from distractions and more typical adolescent concerns. The world shrank to include only what was directly before me, my focus trained entirely on the narrow grid the ducks would be rising from. It was also a place where I could connect with my younger brother. We talked about what was going on at school and about Christmas. We talked about our family, our friends, and life in general. We shared things about ourselves that we'd never discuss at home. In a duck blind, time slowed to a crawl, becoming ultimately meaningless, because there was nowhere else to go and nowhere else we needed to be.

That said, being teenagers meant not much time had to pass before our stomachs started to rumble.

"Hey Laurence," I said, after holding out as long as I could.

"Yeah?"

"You cold?"

"A little."

"How about you go back to the house, maybe warm up for a while, and then bring back some soup and sandwiches?"

"Good idea."

"You know what to do if you hear some shots, right?"

"Yeah. Come back fast, because you probably shot a duck and I'll need to pick it up."

"That's right," I said.

Laurence got back into the dinghy and fired up the motor. I watched him cruise toward land, listening to the ice pinging against the aluminum hull. When he reached the shoreline, he pulled the dinghy out of the water, walked up the big block stairs to the house, and was gone. I turned away and sat on the spackle bucket and kept an eye peeled to the horizon to look for ducks.

I kept scanning for ducks. As any experienced waterman knows, sea ducks behave very differently from other ducks. While a puddle duck such as a mallard or black will circle high up in the sky and look for any sign that reveals something isn't quite right, sea ducks fly low, right above the water. Scaup ducks have a muted blue bill with a black front and a black tail separated by grayish feathers in the middle. When they're flying at the blind right above the water on a cloudy, overcast day like that day was, they were incredibly difficult to spot. If your attention wavered for even a second, they could pass the peaks and troughs of dark bay water and be gone before you could even raise your gun.

I stood up in my tippy blind and looked out at the sea again. I noticed a slight chop, with one wave being a little bit bigger than the others. It wasn't large enough to be a rogue wave, prone to springing out of nowhere, carrying both danger and the promise of damage. That wave was just a little bit bigger than the first and might have come from the wake of a boat motoring around the corner just out of sight. But I didn't hear or see any other boats on the water.

Even so, the waves kept coming at me, slapping up against my blind with steady force. The blind rocked and a sudden swell crested just short of me, tipping over my shotgun from its perch in the corner. It landed with a thud, and then . . .

Boom! . . . Boom! Boom!

Automatics are meant to fire quickly after each pull of the trigger, and when mine hit the deck of the blind, three shells discharged. The safety hadn't held, and I learned later that there was a manufacturing defect that allowed the firing pin to engage on impact.

The percussion of the blast in such a contained area rattled my ears. I couldn't hear a thing and felt totally disoriented. I felt a high-pitched ringing sensation that seemed to emanate from the deepest point of my skull. My balance wavered, almost like I was drunk inside the narrow confines of the blind, which had further amplified the reports thanks to its camouflaged roof. I wound up on the floor of the blind shaking with fear but reassured by the presence of the walls around me. Laurence would be back any minute, and I'd have to tell him that there were no ducks to pick up. At least I'd get some hot soup, though, and that was enough to make me smile.

Boy, was that close, I thought.

The blind was rocking back and forth, and I reveled in the fact that no one would ever know *how* close I'd come to potential disaster. My father was at work, the rest of my family likely out and about except for my grandmother, who seldom left the house. None of them would ever hear about the experience unless I told them, and I suppose at that point I'd be laughing about it. But I wasn't going to tell them, because if I did my mother especially might forbid me from ever going duck hunting again. The embarrassing secret would stay with me, and I resolved to not even tell Laurence.

As a waterman, I knew my next task was to get my body up from the cold deck and back onto my bucket. I looked around for my shotgun and found it facing me from a corner of the blind floor. I put my hands down beside me and went to push up off the floor. But my left leg wouldn't cooperate, wouldn't even move. And when I looked down, I saw why.

That foot was facing in the wrong direction.

2

SHOT

And it was twitching. There was just a trickle of blood, thanks to the frigid air, and I didn't feel any pain. I tried to turn it, but it wouldn't budge. My hands moved, my right leg moved, but not the left with its foot twisted the wrong way around. I heard the ringing in my ears and realized I was trembling from the cold, but otherwise I didn't feel a thing. I lay there on the floor of the blind, recalling the first wave that had rocked the blind and the others that followed. My mind flashed back to the shotgun tipping over and discharging three times, struck by an awful realization in that moment.

I've been shot!

My heart started to beat faster and faster, pounding wildly. I could feel the steady throb in my ears that wouldn't stop ringing from the percussion of the blasts. The blind started to spin around me. My head was pounding too, and my face felt hot. I touched my forehead, and sweat was pouring down over skin that, moments before, had stung with cold in the dank, frigid air. I smelled gunpowder and the stringent scent of salt in the air. I felt something warm soaking my leg but still didn't glimpse any blood spilling onto the deck. The blind continued to rock, and I wasn't sure if that was a result of the waves or my rapidly diminishing hold on consciousness. Yet through it all, the strangest of thoughts formed in my head:

My father is going to kill me!

Band-Aids! I needed Band-Aids, a whole bunch of them to patch this up before my father got home. My father was a stern man with whom I enjoyed, well, let's call it an old-school relationship. His business was all-consuming, and he fretted about that even at home. You could see the consternation and worry on his face every night when he came home, and it would hang there through dinner. He didn't ask us how our days had gone or what we had learned in school, and he didn't have time for things like Little League or Police Athletic League (PAL) football. Like I said, he was old-school, and oftentimes the most any of his kids could get from him then was a head shake and disapproving scowl. I can only imagine how he'd greet the news that I'd shot myself.

There was a big box of Band-Aids in the upstairs bathroom and a lesser assortment tucked in the downstairs bathroom. I'd need to get myself bandaged up before my father had a chance to notice. First, Laurence needed to get his ass back to the blind so I could get home. Where the hell was he? What was taking him so long? He was supposed to come when he heard the shots, but I didn't see him anywhere.

What if he hadn't heard them?

What if he'd sat down and nodded off to sleep?

What if I was stuck here for the rest of the day?

I looked down again at my green rubber boot with the yellow laces pulled tight, facing in the wrong direction. I still didn't see any blood leaking from the wound, which hardly diminished the reality that I'd been shot.

I focused on the shoreline. Much too far away at a quarter mile to swim toward in forty-degree water. I was a good swimmer, and I could have managed that distance in summer months in no time at all. Today, though, I had shirts and sweaters and jackets and gloves and boots to contend with, adding weight and further discouraging a swim through the icy waters.

What other choice did I have? I could take off my clothes and tough it out in the icy currents. But that didn't take into account how I could even make it into the water with my left leg immobile. And how could I make it back to shore through the slosh of ice with the limb dragging behind me?

I thought of Mrs. O'Hara, a friend's mother. She was a wonderful woman who loved to ski and had traveled with her family to a lot of different mountains throughout New England and New York. One winter she took a ski trip to upstate New York. She was driving in the mountains and was coming around a slippery slope when she lost control. She was turning the wheel and pumping the brakes, but the car kept spinning. She was headed for a cliff, about to plummet to her death. Her life flashed before her eyes. She grabbed her rosary beads, clasped them firmly, and prayed. Her car stopped right at the edge, and ever since she had credited those beads with saving her life.

Where were my rosary beads?

They were in my left pants pocket, the same side my shot-up foot was on. I grabbed hold of them and squeezed tight. We were practicing Catholics who went to church every Sunday, and that was about it. After Mass, though, we had our rituals. We'd go to the local bakery to get a pecan pie and the deli to grab Kaiser rolls and a boiled ham. Then we'd go home and have breakfast, after which we'd go out for a boat ride or something, which encompassed basically what passed for a bond with my father. In that perilous moment in the blind, though, I recalled the story of Mrs. O'Hara. If rosary beads had saved her, maybe they could do the same for me.

If I stayed in the blind I would die. If I tried to swim to shore I would drown. I held on to my rosary with all the strength I could muster. I prayed to God to save my life and to help me and all of those around me to make it through this ordeal.

I can do anything with the help of Christ.

I don't know if I said it aloud or if I just thought it, but within a few minutes I saw Laurence at the shoreline pulling our dinghy into the water.

He must have heard the gunshots after all. Duck hunters can normally discern the situation by the number of shots fired. One shot almost always means a dead duck. Two shots usually means that a duck was hit with the first shot and finished off with the second. Three shots almost invariably meant that there are no dead ducks, that the hunter did not lead the ducks enough and shot behind them. Or it could mean that the hunter was firing at ducks that were out of range. Regardless, three shots meant that no ducks were on the water, which may have explained the delay in Laurence's return.

Laurence loaded up the skiff, pulled it into the water, and turned it to face the blind. He dropped the lower unit and propeller into the water, squeezed the ball a few times, and pulled the cord. It fired up easily and he climbed aboard. He probably figured that, after eating lunch, we'd spend another hour or two in the blind, maybe get a few more shots at ducks, and then pick up our decoys and head back in.

The dinghy putted slowly toward the blind. Laurence had it at full throttle, but it was a small dinghy with a small motor. I heard the ice ping off the aluminum hull and watched the bow bob up and down as he motored toward the blind. He tied the dinghy down, started to climb into the blind, and froze when his eyes fell upon me.

"Oh, shit . . . What happened?"

His eyes were wide with shock and terror, and his forehead wrinkled in fear.

"Never mind," I rasped, my mouth bone-dry. "We've gotta get back to shore. I . . . I need your help."

With that, I found the strength to climb over the four-foot platform at the front of the blind and eased myself toward the edge. Laurence joined me on the deck, looped an arm around me, and lowered me into the dinghy. The boot seemed to be the only thing holding my foot to my ankle, and I rolled from the blind into the bow of the dinghy with a flop. Laurence dropped in, fired up the outboard, came about, and headed to shore.

I closed my eyes, suddenly tired. I felt myself nodding off, consciousness ebbing.

"Hey, what are you doing? Wake up! Wake the fuck up!"

I stirred but found myself in a daze. Laurence was still talking, stringing thoughts together I only caught bits and pieces of.

"Stay awake, man! Stay with me! Talk to me! I'm right here! You're going to be fine."

His last words didn't sound very convincing. Not that it mattered. The world had turned soft and cushiony. The swaying of the dinghy made me feel like a baby again, rocking safe and sound. I felt warm, at peace. I just wanted to let myself slip off to sleep.

"No!" Laurence yelled. "I told you to *stay awake*! Open your damn eyes! You hear me? *Open your damn eyes!*"

I realized I was still squeezing the rosary beads in my pants pocket and began drifting again.

"Donald! Donald, we're almost there!"

I fought to open my eyes. The little outboard whined. I saw the shore fast approaching.

"Where's Mom?" I asked Laurence.

"I don't know. Not home."

"Who's home?"

"Nana."

Our grandmother drove an old Ford Falcon. I looked down at my crooked foot and saw blood soaking through my pants leg for the first time.

I felt a thud and heard the sound of the aluminum hull scraping over the rocks, shells, and sand as Laurence ran the skiff onto shore.

Our house was built high above the waterline, and we had about a thirty feet of concrete steps to climb from the shore to reach it. The steps were spread out at different heights and levels, part of the retaining wall that kept the sea from swallowing up our home, and they were going to be a bitch to climb. Incredibly, Laurence practically carried me up the hill, all 115 pounds of him. I could feel his slight frame supporting me, refusing to buckle under the strain of climbing the stairs I never could have managed on my own.

"You gotta get Nana ready to drive me to the hospital, and you've gotta move fast," I told him when we reached the top, baying for breath.

Laurence was dripping with sweat, the exertion showing on his features, and the tips of his blond hair curled at the ends.

"Then go into the shed and get two tomato stakes," I said to him. "Why?"

"I need to use them as crutches. Go! Hurry!"

He sprinted toward the house like an Olympic hurdler and returned quickly with the stakes. They wouldn't fit under my arms, but if I grabbed them on their sides I could push my weight forward, an uneasy motion that would nonetheless allow me to reach the Ford Falcon parked in the driveway.

I had come alert, adrenaline forcing the fatigue from my system. Laurence running on ahead would give my grandmother the time she needed to get ready enough to drive the four-mile distance to nearby St. Francis Hospital; being older, she needed a lot of time to get ready to do anything. Calling 911 wouldn't get help fast enough, at least in our young minds, and I didn't dare wait for an ambulance when my foot was hanging from my ankle. I could only imagine what Laurence was going to say to our grandmother.

Donald got shot and his foot fell off!

The mere thought of those words brought a smile to my face that diminished quickly. I fell into an awkward rhythm and counted my blessings that there was no ice on the ground to waylay me before I reached the driveway.

My grandmother had just emerged from the house when I reached the driveway on my makeshift crutches. She took one look at me using the tomato stakes as crutches but, fortunately, didn't notice the condition of my foot and realize the severity of my injury.

"Let's go," she said, easing her small frame behind the wheel.

Laurence helped settle me in the front passenger seat, then lurched into the back.

My grandmother's approach to driving was deliberate, to say the least. She was determined to make the Falcon last as long as she could, so she tended to baby it, letting the engine warm up before driving off. Much to my consternation, my dire situation did nothing to change that habit.

"Nana!" I pleaded. "*Please!*"

My grandmother's Falcon kicked up smoke from the exhaust pipe as she finally eased it into reverse and backed up slowly onto the street. It seemed to take forever for her to shift the old car into gear and then edge it forward toward the stop sign at the end of our street.

"Please, Nana," I pleaded. "Hurry!"

She gave the car more gas, and we headed off on the drive to St. Francis Hospital.

It would be the four longest miles of my life.

3

ST. FRANCIS

St. Francis Hospital specialized in treating patients with heart conditions. It was a well-known facility, and patients came from far away for treatments, though not necessarily for gunshot wounds. The facility was located on a windy backcountry road and was our closest—our only—option.

At her age, understandably, my grandmother was a cautious driver on even a calm day, which meant she drove with both hands tightly fastened to the wheel. She slowed at every traffic light, stopped at every stop sign, and drove just under the speed limit so she wouldn't get a ticket. The car engine was warm now, so at least the car wasn't sputtering any longer.

I looked down at my foot canted in the wrong direction and saw a trickle of blood dripping out of my pant leg to my grandmother's pristine car mat.

"Please, Nana, go faster," I begged when she didn't risk going through a yellow light. "Hurry up!"

She didn't respond, her focus trained entirely on the road. But she saw me shivering and turned on the heater to take the chill off, and the warmth poured out of the vents. The heat felt good on my face, but all of a sudden, the blood began gushing out from my leg onto the floor mats. I knew we needed to get to the hospital faster than we were going, so out of desperation, I rolled to my left and stuck my right foot on the gas pedal.

"Donald!" she gasped.

"Just steer, Nana. Please, just steer."

I pressed it down to the floorboard while my grandmother worked the steering wheel. The distance started to fly by. I breathed a sigh of relief when St. Francis Hospital came within sight, and we turned into the front entrance of the emergency room.

"Go get a wheelchair," I said to Laurence.

My grandmother opened her door of the coupe so he could squeeze out and run. Moments later he returned with a wheelchair.

I threw open the car door and staggered out into the chair. Nurses and orderlies were gathered at the front entrance when we rolled through the front doors. The first thing I noticed when Laurence wheeled me in was my father standing there; after learning of my accident from Laurence, he'd beaten us to the hospital, thanks to my grandmother's driving. Concern and worry creased his face, but there was no anger. My father was a no-nonsense, take-charge guy. He'd fought in the Battle of the Bulge, which basically marked the end of World War II in Europe, and if there was a problem, he wanted it fixed, preferring to do so himself. Since this problem was clearly out of his hands and in God's, he busied himself with calmly addressing the emergency room doctors and nurses to make sure I would be receiving the best care possible. At one point, he squeezed my hand in an uncommon show of affection and support.

Meanwhile, I was lifted from the wheelchair onto a gurney, while Laurence explained I'd had a shooting accident and my foot had been hit. Two orthopedic surgeons were on call that day and, in a stroke of fortune, it turned out that one of them had been a combat medic in Vietnam who had significant experience with the kind of wound I'd suffered. The nurses began asking me questions, lots of questions, about when was the last time I ate, if I had any allergies to medicine, and how it happened. I was able to answer some of the questions, but I started to feel myself nodding off. Someone began cutting away my pant leg while others removed my clothes.

Amid the human traffic around me, I put my head back on the pillow and closed my eyes. The last thing I remembered was reaching for my rosary beads when the nurses were taking off my coat. They had fallen out of my pocket and onto the gurney. The nurse was surprised, with good reason—how many sixteen-year-old boys carried rosary beads? She may have even been more surprised when a priest arrived and administered last rites to me, out of the very real fear that I would die from blood loss.

The doctors began probing my foot, pressing and prodding to see what was still intact and what was not. A sea of people in medical scrubs surrounded me, some moving away from my gurney only to be replaced by others, yelling and asking for things.

"Need more gauze here STAT!"

"Bring in more saline!"

"Irrigating the wound . . ."

All this transpired while I was being hooked up to beeping monitors and IV lines. There was so much activity around me, I couldn't keep track of all that was happening. I watched the ER team handing things back and forth between them, but I couldn't tell what they were passing around. I had been struggling to hold onto consciousness, but finally I surrendered to the deep sense of fatigue that had settled over me. I pushed my head deep into the pillow and drifted off.

It's a shock to wake up in a strange place and have absolutely no idea or memory of where or why you are there. I looked around and saw nothing familiar. The walls were the color of primer, virtually the same shade as the ceiling. There were institutional windows with institutional metal blinds, the kind that you'd see in any kind of government-owned building like a town hall or a public school. The room couldn't have been any more drab or lifeless than it already was, and when I moved my head from side to side I saw a metal cage designed to keep me in the bed. At the head of the bed were tall, thin metal rods that held lots of different bags full of liquids. Tubes connected the bags to my arms and to my nose, and there were so many that it looked like a spider plant with vines drooping all over a pot.

Okay, I was in a hospital, but why? What had happened? I had no memory of the accident, as if my mind had buried it in the deepest recesses of my consciousness. I was trying to make sense of why people in the room were skirting across the ceiling and walking on the walls, courtesy of the morphine drip easing into my veins. Morphine is one of those drugs that makes you feel light, airy, and hazy. When on morphine you accept that people walking on the ceiling is normal. And it makes you see yourself in a different way, a way that makes even bad news seem good.

I drifted in and out of consciousness, but my first lucid memory was of asking anyone in the room if I was going to die. No one would answer me. I looked around for a familiar face but saw none. There were lots of lights, incredibly bright ones, so bright that they distorted my vision. I also heard voices of men and women that sounded distant and nearby at the same time. Then my head began to pound.

The headache was more like a migraine than a regular headache, pounding with every heartbeat and hammering in the back of my head.

"I . . . I . . . I," I started, unable to complete my thought.

"Are you in pain?" I think it was a nurse who asked me.

My mouth felt dry and pasty. I couldn't speak but must have nodded.

More morphine was administered to reduce the pain, and the headache went away. *This is good, everything is good*, I thought. Then I looked down toward the foot of the bed.

"Hey," I laughed. "What happened to my foot?"

I passed out before I got an answer.

Several days passed before my mind finally cleared enough to recall what had happened, helped greatly by my parents, who filled in the gaps based on what Laurence had told them. I needed help putting the sequence of events together. When certain gaps were filled in, my memory began to return: I learned of the gunshot accident in the duck blind, which prompted me to remember climbing up the stairs, and then making it to my grandmother's Falcon with the tomato stakes acting as crutches. I learned that my grandmother and Laurence had driven me to the hospital, and I recalled my pants being cut away. Layers of detail were added, and as time passed I pieced it all together.

The shock and frigid conditions on the water had cushioned me from the dire nature of my plight, how close I came to my foot having to be amputated. Miraculously, the emergency room doctors and surgeons had managed to save my foot and reattach it to my leg. The blast had torn away a tremendous amount of skin and tissue from my bone, foot, and ankle, so they inserted three metal pins to stabilize the foot. One pin was inserted horizontally just below my knee, a second horizontal pin was inserted below that one for support and stability, and a third pin was placed vertically just below my ankle and above my heel. That last pin replaced damaged cartilage and was responsible for maintaining the connection between my foot and my leg. The doctors couldn't clean all the lead pellets out, so I'd be carrying hundreds of them in my ankle and foot for the rest of my life.

Although I didn't know it at the time, room 312 at St. Francis Hospital would be my home for the next three months. I would live there, I would eat there, and I would sleep there. The doctor installed what looking like scaffolding all around my bed, also known as traction, to keep my leg elevated and immobile. This scaffolding became my new best friend, one I would play with every day. There were weights by the foot of the bed that were attached to my foot, a monkey-grip bar above me that I used to raise and lower my body off the mattress, and enough cables and pulleys to resemble an offshore fishing boat. If someone had told me, a sixteen-year-old young man, that I'd be spending the middle of my high school junior year playing with this jerry-rigged jungle gym, I'd have said they were crazy.

My first order of business was to look at my leg. I couldn't bear to do that, and even if I could, my leg and foot were completely encased in bandages. Since I couldn't see anything, I tried to move my toes. It worked! I could move them down and up, and when I did so I could feel my calf tighten and loosen. Feeling my toes move and my calf tighten made me think that maybe it wasn't as bad as everyone said it was. Maybe I'd be out of there soon, ready to resume my life.

The problem was that I couldn't feel my ankle. When I tried to move it, I felt nothing at all. I could move and feel my toes and my calf, but I couldn't feel anything in between; it was as if my ankle was missing. I'd later learn that I was suffering from extensive nerve, tissue, and vascular damage. There was basically no ankle left; it had, quite literally, been blown apart, and all that remained was bone. A steel pin was all there was holding everything that had once been my lower leg together. So what they basically did was abort the missing ankle altogether and fuse my left foot to the rest of my leg. The idea was to perform the fusion on an angle that would allow me to walk on the tip of my toes over time on that side, since I no longer had an ankle to support me.

I guess I won't be getting out of here soon after all . . .

How could I walk if my ankle didn't move? The stiffness was not only incessant, it was also painful. The doctors explained that while they had saved my foot and were able to constructively reattach it to my leg, the surgery came with a cost. The ligament and tendon damage was so extreme that I faced a long road of rehabilitation ahead.

"How extreme?" I asked a doctor I'd come to recognize, who laid things out for me.

"Well, you'll be able to walk so—"

"What about run?"

He looked at me compassionately. "I was going to say you'll be able to walk, but only with a crutch or cane."

"Forever?"

I think he nodded, but the tears were streaming down my face and I couldn't see through them.

"You should consider yourself fortunate to be alive," the doctor said.

Alive, sure, and, yes, I was grateful for my foot still being attached to the ankle I couldn't feel. But a sixteen-year-old boy stuck using a cane or crutch for the rest of his life?

I cried a lot that day.

And that wasn't all. I had lost a full two inches of height on my left side, and my skeleton would be forever out of alignment. That immediate loss of height would put a tremendous amount of stress and strain on my knees, my hips, my back, and my neck. Add to that the fact that, without the ankle, I'd no longer be able to build any muscle in my left calf, so I also had atrophy to that muscle added to the list of what I was facing. Yes, the surgery on my foot was successful, but I would suffer with the result for the rest of my life.

Technically, I still had a foot, but according to the prognosis, I'd never be able to do any of the things all boys take for granted. My mind instinctively flashed back to my love of hunting, the great times spent on the duck blind where I'd almost lost my foot. I couldn't imagine working my way onto it from our dinghy, couldn't so much as picture how I was going to even get into the dinghy in the first place. I would never be able to do the things that define a waterman. Not fishing, boating, sailing, or hunting. I would never get to dance again, or walk across campus to go to class. I would hobble, I would be in pain, and I would be restricted in everything

I did for the rest of my life. The upside was that if I worked hard and all went well, I would be able to trade the bed for a wheelchair and then the wheelchair for crutches. Small victories as well as small consolation.

I was a long way from having a long-term plan in place, and the doctors and nurses needed to monitor my vitals and progress multiple times each day. Not being able to move meant not being able to perform even the simplest of tasks. I would need help for everything, and I would require full-time, around-the-clock supervision. At this point, going home, going to school, and walking down the aisle to our pew at church all seemed like hopeful visions instead of realities to strive for. Room 312 by the window encompassed my entire world.

I did have roommates, three I clearly recall. There were two older men, both in for open-heart surgery which was St. Francis' real specialty, who were terrific guys and we got along great. One of the things about being in a hospital is that it seems to shrink the distance in years. It didn't matter that I was a kid and both of them could have been my father, or even my grandfather—our plights had placed us on common ground. Sandwiched in between these two men, though, was a thirteen-year-old boy named Jeffrey, in for a simple knee operation, who was a pain in the ass in that he wouldn't stop buzzing for the nurses. A piece of paper on the floor . . . *buzz!* A lunch tray he was finished with . . . *buzz!* Get his bed elevated . . . *buzz!* You name it and Jeffrey had a *buzz* for it. I told him off a couple of times and couldn't help think that this little whiner was the same age as my younger brother, who had saved my life.

"What's wrong with you?" I barked at him once. "Don't you know the nurses have better things to do?"

He shut up for a while, but not long enough.

My body became a pincushion as blood was drawn daily for testing to be sure that no disease had set in. After a while there weren't too many veins left available, the lot of them already taken by the

IV antibiotics, painkillers, and whatever else they were giving me. Gone were all my regular activities like showering or getting up to brush my teeth. I couldn't even relieve myself without a bedpan. These nurses visited me several times a day to remove my smock and give me a sponge bath, clinically and without emotion, moving my body into different positions to prevent bedsores.

Here I was, a sixteen-year-old young man being treated like a nursing home patient. In my former life, a normal day consisted of waking up, going to school, then coming home and doing homework. After a while, I'd take a break from studying to listen to music and walk down to the kitchen to grab a snack. After homework and studying I'd either watch TV or grab the phone and call friends to make plans for the upcoming weekend. My parents would tell me to pick up after myself, to clean my room, and to follow up on my chores. I'd go to Driver's Ed and study to get my license, with an eye toward borrowing the car and becoming a free man. That had been my life; now my life stretched only as far as the contours of my hospital bed.

Nobody remembers what it's like to be an infant, the notion of being fed, bathed, and having diapers changed. That was the life I was now living, although it would be something I'd never forget. I, like everyone else, had taken so much for granted for so long, something I resolved never to do again.

Drugs relieved the pain but numbed my thoughts and my feelings too. My mind was lucid enough to realize, though, that the doctors weren't offering any hope with my prognosis.

Some people were telling my parents I deserved the injury because I was out killing animals. But I wasn't going to give in to them or my condition. My only solace was my resolution to overcome my injury and prove the doctors wrong. I would climb out of my bed and walk out of St. Francis Hospital without a cane or crutches. I would show everyone that I was as tough as nails, maybe even tougher.

But life had other ideas.

4

SAVING MY LEG

My resolve was beaten back by tests that showed something was very wrong, and the doctors were called in to investigate. By now my arms had so many tracks from blood tests, IVs, and assorted drips that I looked like some junkie. More tests were taken, and the results came back as bad as it gets:

Gangrene.

This life-threatening disease can develop when considerable amounts of body tissue die as a result of an injury or infection. Thanks to the shooting accident, I was suffering from both and, in the midst of my resolve to recover, had to confront the most awful reality imaginable.

I might lose my foot.

Gangrene as severe as mine was commonly treated by amputation. All of a sudden, a cane or crutches didn't sound too bad after all. How could I walk if I didn't have a foot? This happened just a short few weeks after awakening to find that my foot, at the very least, was still part of my leg. Now I faced the prospect of losing it altogether.

Even in the modern age, treating gangrene was a complex procedure and one that wasn't always successful. If the blood vessels could be reengineered to transport oxygen, nutrients, and antibiotics to the area, my foot might be saved for the second time. But quite a few complications could result from the treatment, since the bacteria was prone to spread to other healthy tissue, leading the body to have a toxic reaction, a shock that could be lethal. Even if they amputated my foot, there was no guarantee I'd survive, because the disease could have spread throughout my body and infected other organs.

Instead of being confronted with living the rest of my life disabled, I was confronted with losing it altogether. And, unlike musing with the resolve to fully recover no matter what it took, I was utterly helpless against the disease ravaging my body. I was either going to lose my foot or my life, and I stood a decent chance of losing both—those were the prospects I was facing.

Nighttime was the worst, after my family and the doctors went home. My roommate and most of the patients on my wing quieted down and went to sleep. All the televisions were turned off. It was dark outside, dark in the wing beyond, and dark in my room, leaving me alone with my thoughts. Up until that point I had felt helpless in the face of my limitations, but that didn't remotely compare to this new level of despair.

What did I have to live for? Where was the hope?

If you've ever been in a hospital ICU, then you know what it's like to be immersed in a world both bland and sterile. The smell of thick, canned air fills your world amid a landscape where even the windows are kept closed to ward off the potential spread of disease. The bitter scent of cleaning disinfectant hangs everywhere, diminishing at times but never fading away altogether. Or maybe that scent can be better described as the residue of the pain and misery that permeates the wing. Maybe I wasn't smelling disinfectant at all so much as the collective sense of hopelessness. The tubular lighting shone upon a bleak world of neutral-colored paint, cold metal door frames, and drop ceilings that shrink the world. Some patients recovered and walked out the front door; others didn't and were rolled away to funeral homes.

At night, the darkness and the hospital smell became all-encompassing as I replayed in my mind that day's frustrating prognoses from the doctors who examined me on a regular basis.

"We're not sure."

"We need to wait and see."

"We'll take each day as it comes."

"Every day presents new challenges; every day presents new solutions."

The lack of a decision, direction, or plan of action was more maddening than anything. Not knowing what was going to happen, not having a concrete plan caused me to sink into a deep and profound depression.

Depression gets into your head, and then it goes into your heart. It tests the resolve of even the hardiest and most stoic, and it does so during the quiet time of the night. Every night I stewed in my own miserable thoughts until I passed out just before sunrise. Without fail, my roommate would awaken, fully rested from a night's sleep, and the nurse would come in for her regularly scheduled morning visit. I'd wake up at that point, ragged from fear, ravaged by depression, and thoroughly exhausted to hear her morning words, "How did you sleep?"

The doctors finally began to coalesce around a prognosis, and it was not encouraging. They were openly stating that I would never walk normally again, deepening my depression. To their credit, the doctors never gave me any false hope.

When they changed the bandages, they found that the infection was spreading and the surrounding tissue was not healing, a worst-case scenario. The pins were holding my foot in place, but my foot was beginning to die. My circulation was poor, and the gangrene was cannibalizing my healthy tissue. The pain was excruciating. Every time the cleaning man entered the room to spread more sanitizer on the linoleum floor, his bucket would hit the weights next to the bed, and the reverberation of metal on metal raced through the cables to my foot and into the pins. That pain left me gasping in agony and sweating, a steady run of tears flowing down both cheeks. The pain shot up to my knee, and my entire leg throbbed deep into the bones for hours on end. Everything felt raw, and it never really ebbed. Nurses administered more morphine, while the doctors shook their heads.

The decision was made for me to undergo another round of surgery. When you hear that you'll never walk again, and you're surrounded by pain and humiliation, that's the last thing you want to hear, especially when there was no guarantee the surgery would do anything but delay the inevitable. I would be going into the operating room in a weakened mental, emotional, and physical state. I was beaten down to the point where I'm not sure I even cared anymore. I was, like, *Whatever.*

But why me?

In addition to surgery on my ankle, I'd had pigskin grafted into place to help speed the healing. The problem was it hadn't taken, so in the next round of surgery I was going to have skin taken from my buttocks and grafted in place instead, something I realized represented a significant setback. In order to potentially save my foot, I had to submit to a procedure that would dramatically set back my recovery. It would cause me greater pain, extend my period of rehabilitation significantly, and create additional complications. Since I had no ambulatory movement, I would be forced to lie on the open wounds that came from the skin graft. No one could write a script capturing this kind of misery.

The consultation and discussions continued so that the doctors could be sure they were going in the right direction. Tests were performed more frequently, and the results were studied and reviewed. I wondered out loud whether this might be some kind of experimental, unproven procedure, rendering me nothing more than a human guinea pig for doctors to poke, prod, and slice.

My depression grew even deeper. Time crawled. The period from sundown until sunup seemed like an eternity, and the morphine was all that helped me get through the long, endless hours. I'd take to studying the steady drip of the drug into my veins, picturing it taking the edge off my pain while able to do nothing about my underlying condition. Days and weeks blended together to the point where I felt completely and totally lost; I normally didn't even know what day of the week it was. My family, the nurses, and the doctors did their best to quiet my nerves, but I had reached a breaking point from which there seemed to be no return. I had always thought of hospitals as places where people went to get better from what was ailing them.

Not me, though.

When I closed my eyes, I saw a slow, painful death in my future. The best thoughts I could muster were of a sedentary life where my current experience became the norm. I had already come apart physically, and now the spiritual and emotional parts of me were following.

Everything begins with a decision. Smokers wake up one morning and decide that they have had enough of cigarettes and quit. Overweight folks hit a similar breaking point and commit to losing weight. I reached that breaking point, where I could concede—give up altogether—or grit my teeth and fight.

One morning, when the nurses came in, I made a pronouncement: "I'm going to walk again."

One of the nurses simply smiled, but the other squeezed my shoulder.

"Yes, you will."

I was done with mourning and lamenting. I focused on what seemed impossible at the time, because it represented a return to normalcy in my life. You can't grab something unless you reach for it, and that was what I was doing. Reaching for a miracle and stretching as high up on my toes as I needed in order to snare it. All this would not defeat me. I would accept nothing less than a full recovery. I told the doctors if they rebuilt my foot, I would walk on it out of St. Francis. I started counting the days and hours to my surgery, filled with renewed hope and even certainty that it was going to work. I pitched my fears out the window, and then my depression with the next toss.

Similar to the first time I'd gone under the knife, I didn't remember anything about the surgery until a while after it was over. The doctors and nurses were optimistic, pleased with how it had gone. They had removed a lot of the damaged tissue, along with the disease, and had further rebuilt the veins to strengthen circulation. They also removed a great number of the shotgun pellets they'd missed in the initial surgery, although they couldn't get to them all.

There was hope, enough to reinforce my new attitude. Through the incredible pain, even more of it now thanks to all the skin that had been cut from my buttocks, I focused on nothing more than walking again. I'd look down at my bandages through a morphine haze and will my foot to heal.

I will walk, I told myself, over and over. I chanted it as if I were a Benedictine monk. And then, like a miracle, over the course of a few weeks my prognosis changed and the good started to even up with the bad. Major milestones for most sixteen-year-olds was to get a driver's license, find a good summer job, and go to the prom. For me it was being able to sit up in my bed. The significance of that went beyond moving from a horizontal into an upright position because, more importantly, I did it on my own. Sitting up in bed was the first independent activity that I did in weeks, and I was overwhelmed. It felt like the greatest feat I'd ever accomplished in my life.

And then it hit me: How much of my life did I take for granted? That was sort of odd thinking for a kid my age, but it became important, if not critical, to my recovery. That otherwise minor achievement rekindled my spirits and gave me hope. It empowered me to excel in my rehabilitation. It made me want to eat even the nastiest hospital food to get stronger. Most importantly, it was an affirmation of my original goal:

I will walk.

After a few weeks I was tasked with moving from the bed to a chair. My nurses and the orderlies broke down the concept of "walking" into steps. I thought it was a bizarre concept. I had crawled and then walked as a baby, yet I never really considered the concept of "how to walk" before. At home I'd simply go from my bed to the chair, but now I had to focus on sitting up, moving my legs, swinging them over the bed, placing them on the floor next to the walker, then using my upper-body strength to lift myself up. I placed all my weight on my right leg and could feel the blood flow down through my legs until I felt light-headed. I still couldn't put any weight on my left leg, but I could hop with the walker supporting me. When I hopped those first steps and moved across the floor to the chair, turned around, and sat down, I was overwhelmed with joy. This simple act made me feel like I had climbed Mount Everest and left me thinking that if I could do this, someday I would walk, even run, and live a normal life again.

Doctors could see the change in me and followed suit. Gone were the comments like, "He'll never walk again." My optimism was contagious, and their doubt was replaced with enthusiasm for the steady progress I was making, literally one step at a time. The first time I heard the doctor say, "Wow, I can't believe that he's doing this already," my spirits soared, reinforcing my conviction.

I started standing, and hopping in smoother fashion with a walker. An incredible achievement, yes, but I wouldn't be satisfied until I could stand upright and walk on my own. Crutches, actually, became my best friend because they facilitated at least a semblance of normalcy and independence, albeit with the pain in my shoulders and especially my underarms to deal with. I had a hard road ahead of me, each successive step in recovery more challenging than the last. My young, formerly healthy body had weakened, even atrophied in places, so I couldn't hold myself up for very long. By the time I reached the chair I was exhausted, but it didn't matter. I focused on the fact that I had done it instead of how hard it had been. Moments like that strengthened me, reinforced the reality that I could recover based on force of will alone. Every day left me with something new to build on. More steps, less pain, a faster recovery, less morphine. Suddenly I was able to hop with the walker's support across the entire length of the room that had once seemed as long as a football field.

My next milestone was probably the most significant for rebuilding my morale and affirming my recovery: I was ready to use the bathroom alone. My foot had not healed enough to take a shower, but I was able to use the restroom without assistance. The fact that I could combine walking with a trip to the bathroom meant that I no longer needed a bedpan. I felt a freedom, a sense of independence I hadn't felt in months. It was truly amazing how such a simple act could be so exhilarating. I had learned to take great pleasure and pride in the simplest of accomplishments.

My doctors and nurses were continually amazed by my progress, and that only fueled my desire to push myself more. I felt my depression melting away and being replaced with confidence and determination. When the sun set every night, I no longer felt despair closing in on me but instead was exhausted from all the rehab and fell fast asleep. And as time passed, I was no longer bothered by the nurse's question, "How did you sleep?" Because my answer had changed.

"Like a rock," I'd tell her.

And before long I'd be facing my greatest test yet: walking on my own.

5

THE VIEW
FROM OUTSIDE

M y recovery went better than expected. As I gained weight and strength, my coordination started to return and my foot was healing quickly. One of the benefits of being so young was that, after the initial setbacks, my body responded very well to treatment.

One day in the hospital I asked for a present: I wanted to be taken outside in a wheelchair.

As a boy who considers himself to be a waterman, I loved being surrounded by nature, so being stuck in a hospital room really drained me. The hospital's colors, smells, and confinement made me feel like I was in prison, and looking out the windows along the wall wasn't enough. The sunny days picked up my spirits, while the cloudy, rainy days caused my depression to resurface. But things were different now, because when I gazed out the window I could picture myself outside.

In just a month I went from learning to sit up to walking with assistance. I had earned the right to ask for something special, and going outside was all I wanted.

It was the first time in months that I saw something other than my room, and everything seemed new and refreshing, from the smiling faces of people in the hallways to something as simple as the elevator bell. I was so excited the moment my nurse rolled my wheelchair onto the elevator and we descended to the ground floor. The jolt hurt a bit, but I didn't care and wasn't about to show it. There were more important things to consider.

I was going outside.

I can't remember a time when the air smelled as fresh as it did that day. It was clean and cold, and though it was still winter, there was a hint of spring's warmth. White, feather-light snow was all around, and that added to the overall crispness, with certain melting in the near future. An apt metaphor for what I was feeling, my mood having gone from the depths of winter to the promise of spring. The trees were all bare and there were no birds singing, but I didn't care because I had just traded the metal trapeze for a taste of freedom. I could not take deep-enough breaths of the fresh, clean air or enjoy the moisture and the cold any more than I already was.

Sometimes, when I step outside to this day into comparable weather, I'm transported back to that day in the wheelchair.

I sat in my wheelchair soaking in the natural light, the brisk air, and looking out at things that were not man-made. This was what God created. And that thought led me to consider everything that had been going on with my foot, as well as with my recovery, not just physically but also spiritually. My spiritual journey had proved to be even more far-reaching than my physical one, and much more complex as well. No matter the degree to which my leg healed, my spirit had evolved to a level that most never attain until adulthood, if at all. I had learned not to take the simple things, anything really, for granted. Like going outside during the final throes of winter, carrying the coming of spring on the air. In that moment, I knew there were things I might never be able to do again physically, but I had developed my spirit, my very soul, in a way that would last me for the rest of my life.

Religion was an integral part of my family's life. As a Catholic, I began going to church as an infant, was baptized, served as an altar boy, and went to Catechism before being confirmed. In the span of my sixteen years, I could count on one hand the times that we, as a family, missed Mass. We lived a devoted, spiritual life. Practicing our faith was as much a part of our lives as sitting down to an evening meal, going to work, or going to school.

Until you're faced with a catastrophic, life-altering event, you tend to lose yourself in mindless day-to-day routines that leave you fretting about stuff that doesn't add up to much when compared to the bigger picture near-tragedy reveals. I would never again be the same person who was wheeled into St. Francis to ultimately spend three months in a hospital bed. Our worlds move in a very planned, regimented, and regular way through the usual milestones of school, jobs, and family. Life for us continues on its path, and there are normally few interruptions or disruptions that leave us straying for very long, unless we're pushed off that path as hard as I was.

The experiences that rock this particular boat are the ones that fall outside that normal, expected rhythm of life and violate the order of time. Terminal illnesses, for example, remain one of life's mysteries that cause many to question their principles and faith. Or financial calamity, like job loss, that causes unspeakable harm to a family, like losing their home. Take it from me, though: whoever said when you don't have your health, you've got nothing was right.

The more mundane, day-to-day accidents of fate can be as simple as a cut bad enough to need stitches, breaking a bone by falling from a ladder, or a minor car accident. The more severe ones, on the other hand, violate the natural order and throw life into chaos. Experiences like that challenge our way of living as well as thinking, from how we feel about life to our connection with the universe.

But to question God, you first have to believe in Him.

During my time in the hospital, I asked God repeatedly, "Why is this happening to me?" I wanted to know what I had done to deserve this pain, what I was supposed to learn from it, and what I needed to do to be granted relief. That first day outside, as I sat in my wheelchair appreciating the fresh air, I still sought answers to those questions.

Hunting is a sport for millions of Americans, just like fishing, boating, skydiving, and scuba diving, but not for me that day. Maybe I could have built a rack in the blind so my shotgun wouldn't have fallen over. Yes, I had exercised caution, but there was no way I could have known about the manufacturing defect that had caused the gun to fire. Sure, there were countless things I could have done differently, but the issue for me now was what I was going to do about it. How could I use the experience to make me into a better boy and then man?

Up until my accident, my faith had been unquestioning. All my church and religious activities were set up on the calendar literally or figuratively. They were not to be missed. All other activities and events in my family had to revolve around our spiritual life, which went hand in hand with our family life. I never questioned, I just followed the pattern. And that was the lesson that I believe I needed to learn for myself and not take for granted from the tongues of others.

My accident caused me to go through a wide range of emotions. To call those emotions a roller-coaster ride would be to trivialize my feelings. I went from shock in the duck blind to survival mode instantly. My grandmother and Laurence rushed me to a hospital that specialized in heart ailments, not gunshot wounds. Of all the doctors who happened to be on rotation that day, the one who saw me was a former Vietnam veteran with extensive experience handling gunshot wounds. I was told I'd lose my foot. I was told I'd never walk again. I was told that gangrene might very well take my life. And yet there I was, sitting outside in the crisp air with the road to recovery as plain as the one that ran before St. Francis.

Throughout my ordeal I questioned everything about faith. I went from sort of a mandatory belief in God and our Savior Jesus Christ to a rejection of everything that had to do with anything I had learned or believed. And therein lay the great dichotomy I was facing: when my future looked bleak, my faith disappeared; when my prognosis improved, my faith was restored. What kind of faith is that? I believe the message I needed to learn from this was that I had to embrace and accept my faith without preconditions and not see believing as a transaction between me and God. That would have been an especially heavy lift for the sixteen-year-old boy who'd been wheeled into the hospital, but not so for the sixteen-year-old boy who was wheeled out.

My attitude toward faith changed again. It became as much a part of my life as my next breath. I realized that I couldn't just call on God to fix something that was broken or not right. I couldn't consider myself a spiritual man if I were to complain when things were bad or attempt to dictate through prayer what I wanted to have done. I had to embrace the concept that God has a vision and a plan for me and for my life, and that I would live through the good times as well as the bad times, just as He prescribed. I could fixate on the ordeal I had suffered, or I could learn to enjoy the pleasures of something as simple as breathing fresh, clean air amid a freshly fallen snowpack. I had no desire to look back toward the depths of depression, fear, and intense pain I had suffered. Instead, I chose to look ahead. I still had an incredible amount of work to do in order to achieve my goal of walking, but now I felt I had found the mindset I needed. I was about to face the new and different pain of recovery and return to life—pain, in other words, toward a purpose that I would embrace as much as I had grimaced in the aftermath of my surgeries. I was going to replace the morphine drip with the spiritual variety.

Bring on my recovery! I was ready to face that and anything else life had to throw at me.

6

FIRST STEPS

I was dismissed from the hospital on a cold, gray late-March day in 1978, after precisely twelve weeks and six days. I watched my mom sign a slew of papers so that I could be released. It seemed to take forever, almost like my grandmother's drive to St. Francis in her Ford Falcon.

Finally, my mom wheeled me out the front door, then packed me, my wheelchair, and my crutches into the car, and away we went. I carried practically a book's worth of instructions for my recovery and rehabilitation that I intended to follow precisely on doctor's orders or risk a return to a place I never wanted to see again.

Being in a car and seeing the outside world pass by made me feel like an infant taking their first steps or a young child riding a bike without training wheels. Except for that one foray outside, I had seen nothing but the sanitized interior of the hospital for several months. Even though the day was cloudy, it couldn't have been brighter to me. When you move from a very slow and controlled environment into a faster-paced one with a lot of additional stimulation, the effects are dizzying. Under normal circumstances, it's not hard for a person's brain to handle people talking while the radio is playing when driving past a constant stream of buildings and trees and signs and traffic lights. But when all you've seen are bland white walls and gray window frames for months on end, increased activity can prove overwhelming. Within minutes I was dizzy from looking out the window, and I was thankful that the ride back home was a short one along that same four-mile stretch my grandmother had covered in her Ford Falcon. Things that I had taken for granted, like piling into the car and cranking the radio and looking around, now overloaded me with sensory input. Normal wasn't normal anymore.

The feeling of arriving home was incomprehensible. When I looked at our house and the driveway and the stairs that went down to the water, I could only think of the last time I'd been there three months ago. That was enough to induce what felt like a panic attack in me, catching me in the grip of fear and dread. My last memory of home was when I feared I would lose my life, or my foot. My already spinning head fogged up, and I knew that the only way I could get through it was to push those feelings down deep and not give in to the sense of anxiety threatening my psyche.

Something was tearing at me, and I knew I couldn't just blow past my accident and move on. Even though I was only sixteen, I had to face my fears in order to get through this, face them down. Crutching myself up the steps and getting inside the trusty confines of my house, with all the familiar sights, smells, and sounds, relieved a measure of the tension tightening inside me, but I knew the sense of fear I had felt would return.

Beyond the front door, I looked around the kitchen, the living room, and the dining room. Although nothing was remodeled, things appeared different. Structurally and furnishings-wise, my home was exactly as I left it, from the paintings on the walls to the pictures on the mantel to the drapes and the couches. Then I realized it was *me* who was different. You can't go through an experience like I had endured without it changing every facet of your existence, starting with the way you think. Nothing was the same and never would be again, because I was a much different person than I'd been prior to climbing into my grandmother's car for the drive to St. Francis.

Entering the house, I could see the living room windows that looked out over the bay where the accident had occurred. It was kind of like returning to the scene of the crime, but all I could think about was how much I wanted to get out there and hold my Franchi shotgun again. Our poodle Mimi greeted me with all the excitement and enthusiasm you'd expect, and fortunately, at only about twenty-five pounds, she wasn't much of a threat to topple me over.

Teenagers spend an incredible amount of time in their bedrooms, because a kid's bedroom is the one room in the house where they can make it into exactly what they want. Unfortunately, with my leg in a cast, I wouldn't be able to climb the stairs to my room, so my mother set up a makeshift bedroom for me on the first floor, turning the den into my bedroom and denying me the respite my room upstairs would have provided. Those stairs became my Mount Everest to glance at longingly with an eye on climbing someday. It might take me a while to reach the summit, but gazing up the length of those stairs over and over and over again provided fresh motivation to commit myself to my rehab. Whatever it took to reach the top, I was going to do it.

Then the parade began. A steady stream of people came to visit, the first wave consisting of my parents' friends, neighbors, and others from the community. They came by to show support, to express their sorrow for all the pain and suffering I was feeling, and to wish me well for a speedy recovery. They'd sneak in different types of foods that weren't necessarily keeping with the strict diet I was still on, and they'd catch me up on different events that were going on around school, church, and town. I might have stopped moving, but the world hadn't. My life in the hospital had been so insular, I'd barely considered anything beyond its blank walls. Every visitor was kindhearted and tried their best to keep my spirits high by continuing to connect me with the outside world.

There was plenty of time to think, because I was alone much of the day. I wasn't able to go to class, so I'd wake up, have breakfast, and then engage in a series of activities with my mother, starting with the long process of changing my dressings. She'd remove the gauze wrapped around an open section of my hard cast that went from my foot to my knee to expose the wound, which leaked and oozed constantly. Then she'd unwind yard after yard of Ace bandages and curl them to be used again. Next, she removed the soiled gauze and the pads that, because of their direct contact with the skin grafts, were anything but pretty. Finally, my mom would cleanse my wound, let it air for a while, and then repack my leg in antibiotic cream, new gauze, and new wrappings to cover the hole.

Aside from that I had long stretches of time alone. I spent that time listening to music and watching television, and looked forward to the day I'd able to walk on my own two feet again—well, at least one. I wasn't able to put any weight at all on my left leg because, without an ankle, it wasn't stable and would have collapsed all the delicate repairs my surgeons had made. That meant I had to learn a whole new way of walking.

My high school arranged for my teachers to provide private tutorials for me, covering the same lessons they'd covered with my classmates each day. I really looked forward to these sessions, because they broke up the monotony of the day. With no excuse not to do my homework, I became a diligent student and actually produced the best grades of my life. Sympathy might have been a factor, sure, but my confinement left me enjoying anything that distracted me from the limitations imposed upon me.

Afternoons, after my tutoring sessions, brought a different kind of visitor in the form of my classmates. Word about my accident spread through all the school districts like wildfire, and soon thereafter I was visited by my immediate friends. Most of them had an odd fascination with my accident, one that is common when pain and tragedy strikes high school kids. There are lots of movies and books that delve into the subject of young life cut short, and in a strange way I had become part of that culture. Call it fascination or morbid curiosity, but everyone seemed to want to connect with me now that I had been shot.

I don't know that any high school kid has the presence of mind to know where he stands among his peers. Some kids were really popular because of their achievements in sports while others were outstanding because they were smart or creative or musically inclined. I always thought that I was somewhere in the middle, never really on the leading edge of popularity but also not way in the back. Some days when I went to school I was instantly recognized while on other days I was simply ignored. What a difference an accident like this makes: the floodgates of popularity were opened.

I experienced a newfound fame that was about as confusing to me as the accident itself. I felt it a little bit at the hospital, but far more when I returned home: kids I'd never even interacted with before were suddenly sitting in my living room. I knew some of them from elementary and middle school, but after that we'd gone our separate ways. There were three high schools in the area: Catholic ones for both boys and girls, along with our local town high school for both where most kids went. I was a junior at the Catholic boys high school, so I hadn't seen a great many of my visitors from public school for years, other than a passing glance or nod in town. There wasn't a lot of mingling going on. We'd say hi every now and again, but that was it. I didn't even think they knew where I lived, let alone find their way into my home.

Then I realized they were visiting me because they cared. These were some of the most popular kids in town, the athletes and kind of kids who got voted class president and maybe went on to play lacrosse, basketball, or another sport in college. They came back regularly, demonstrating to me how sometimes it takes a tragedy in life to bring people together, and that kind of positivity kept me upbeat through the long weeks I spent all day in my wheelchair with my leg elevated to prevent it from oozing and to keep the swelling down.

The flow of kids visiting me continued until dinner. Another surge came, typically, after dinner and stayed until bedtime. They wanted to know how I was feeling, what the pain was like, and what my future held. Then we'd start talking about other things: our likes and dislikes, things we did when we weren't in school, what we really thought about our teachers and other classmates, and our dreams for the future. We'd talk about fears, and God and religion, and why certain things happen to some people and not to others. We'd go back and forth on a wide variety of topics, and after a few weeks something occurred to me: I had become good friends with kids I never would have otherwise.

At sixteen, I was telling these kids "I love you," which blew their minds, since it was hardly normal teenage vernacular. But having narrowly escaped the clutches of amputation or death, I was no longer a normal teen. An experience like that stays with you, and you're no longer afraid to express your true feelings.

Now, we no longer simply passed each other in the hallways, because we were different. We knew more about each other than ever before. We had conversations that were meaningful, bonding, and I realized that we were maturing together. The strange part was that I would never have spent any time with them if it weren't for my accident, the irony of which I've never failed to appreciate. It turned out the popular kids, jocks and otherwise, were really no different than me.

In high school, typically, everyone followed his or her calling, whether it was sports or acting or music, and for the most part those groups did not intermingle. Basketball players hung out with basketball players, band members with other band members, and so on and so on. My accident had happened while I was pursuing my passion for duck hunting, which meant I didn't fit in neatly with any group. The accident, though, had transcended all the typical high school bullshit. I'd had so many of the kids who came to visit—and ultimately became my friends—so wrong. They weren't stuck up or boastful; they were just like I was, only they had different interests that had previously kept us apart.

Once in a while, I still pull out the journal I kept during that time to see the get-well cards that people had sent or left after a visit. There were hundreds of them. If you asked me before the accident if I thought that there were hundreds of people who cared about me, my answer would have been a definitive no. I was proved wrong by the parade of visitors who came to visit me. Call that overwhelming sense of love and support the silver lining in the cloud of my accident.

I would be different for the rest of my life. I wasn't crippled, thank God, but there were many things that I'd never be able to do again, like mountain climb, run marathons, join the military, or hike. To be fair, some of these, like marathon running, wasn't ever something I wanted to do, but the important point is that I wouldn't be able to even if I had wanted. I had to learn to handle the loss of possibility.

It was up to me, though, to determine how much I was going to lose. And as I grew stronger, I resolved to make myself back into the same boy who had motored out to the blind that fateful morning in a dinghy with his brother.

But it wasn't going to be easy.

7

STAYING ALIVE

I had a clear goal to focus on: to be able to climb the stairs so I could return to my bedroom. I didn't like sleeping, and living, in the den. Climbing those stairs became my white whale, and I'd spend long intervals at the foot of the staircase, peering upward and visualizing myself crutching up to my room. I took living in the den as a sign of weakness, which meant getting back into my bedroom would be a sign of strength. Everyone was saying I wouldn't be able to manage that task for a long time, something that made me redouble my efforts in order to prove them wrong.

My mother, to her credit, was a fighter like me. She refused to accept my plight and began taking me to a parade of specialists in search of some magic remedy that would make me whole again. I dreaded those trips because of how hard it was for me to get in and out of the house, as well as in and out of the front seat of her red Monte Carlo, which was a struggle every time. One of my three sisters would always come along since our forays took us mostly into New York City where either my mom or my sister would help me out of the car and into the building, while the other went to park the car in parts unknown.

One of the specialists we saw put me on supplements and vitamins to help make me stronger. While most other visits produced no
answers at all, including one with a doctor who specialized in ankle
replacements, for which it turned out I wasn't a good candidate, an
appointment with a prosthetics specialist proved very beneficial. I
wasn't going there to discuss being fitted with a full prosthesis, but
that didn't stop him from pulling up his pants leg to reveal his own
prosthetic leg that had replaced the one he'd lost in a motorcycle accident. His point, I think, was to demonstrate that my situation was
more one of management than rehabilitation, because there wasn't
any rehab that could strengthen an ankle that wasn't there anymore.

Instead, this doctor replaced my hard cast with a much more
efficient, custom-made plastic cast made of many of the same com-
ponents as his prosthetic leg. It was flesh colored, so wearing it made
me look something like a department store mannequin. The plastic
cast was constructed with a panel that could be lowered to expose
my wound in more convenient fashion, and that proved to be a god-
send to my mom's efforts to constantly keep the wound clean. I was
actually fitted with a series of these casts, needing a new one to keep
up with the reduction of swelling in my foot. That meant taking a lot
of measurements, but it was worth it, and I greeted each replacement
as a sign I was improving.

Once I was able to trade the wheelchair for crutches and return
to my bedroom, I found another goal in attending the junior prom,
less than a month away at that point. Not only did I want to go,
not only did I want to dance, I wanted to do so with a cane instead
of crutches. The support of the crutches helped teach me a whole
new way of walking with my foot canted off to the side so I couldn't
put any pressure on it. I dragged more than lifted it and disciplined
myself to never, *never* put any weight on it. I walked like a duck.

Counting the days to the junior prom, I began practicing with a
cane, at first under my mother's supervision but eventually on my
own. I'd walk the length of the downstairs back and forth, finally

gaining the confidence to work my way around tighter areas represented by chairs. This was as close as I came to a formal rehabilitation regimen.

Meanwhile, I had a weight set, dumbbells, heavy bag, and Universal weight machine in my basement. All that crutching had already built up my shoulders, and the Universal had a dip station to continue that strengthening process. I obviously couldn't do any lower-body exercises, but my upper body blew up, and I built a really strong chest and arms that was vital psychologically to make up for the fact that my left foot was useless.

I could barely sleep the night before the prom. My mother didn't want me to go, afraid I'd do something that would set me some or all the way back again. She wasn't wrong. I always had a scab over the wound and the slightest contact risked breaking it, which could lead to another bout of infection. Ultimately, she acquiesced and I think it was my father who changed her mind and talked her into letting me go. He recognized the work ethic I'd been displaying and was a man firmly of the opinion that hard work needed to be rewarded. He was a businessman and veteran of World War II, no stranger to adversity and risk, and knew there'd come a point where I'd have to test myself. So why not the night at the junior prom?

My parents rented a limousine for me and a group of friends along with our dates, and we had dinner at Benihana before heading over to my high school where the junior prom was being held in the gym. One of the kids sharing the limo was my friend Jordan, the son of the woman who'd given me the rosary beads I'd clutched through my pants pocket over the duration of my ordeal on the bay after shooting myself.

I achieved my goal of attending the prom with a cane and found the support from my classmates to be overwhelming. Here I was, a pretty innocuous kid who'd blended into the scenery for most of high school, and now I had become the scenery. Mr. Popularity. And I achieved another of my goals when I danced; well, it was actually more of a wiggle back and forth, thanks to my not being able to put any weight on my left foot, but I still felt like John Travolta from the recently released *Saturday Night Fever*. And like him, that night on the dance floor I was staying alive, dancing to Fleetwood Mac singing the especially appropriate "Don't Stop," along with the band Heart and, of course, the Bee Gees. Unlike Travolta, though, as "Stayin' Alive" opens, there wasn't much I could do to use my walk. There wasn't much I could do that night as far as slow dancing either, but neither could anyone else, given the close watch being paid by the nuns and brothers.

The triumph I felt from that evening didn't last long, though. A few weeks after the prom, my mom didn't like what she saw upon changing my dressing.

"It looks like it might be infected," she said.

We went straight to the doctor, who, sure enough, diagnosed me as having come down with another case of gangrene.

Ughhhhhhh . . .

Knowing what was coming left me utterly deflated. I'd need another skin graft, which meant another patch taken from my butt and all the pain that entailed. And then I wouldn't be able to move and would be bedridden for a week to ten days. It was so discouraging, so mentally deflating. I started to fear that this was going to become the norm of my life, periods of improvement rotating with inevitable setbacks that would render me immobile again.

Fortunately, that stretch passed quickly, and I was able to return to working out in the basement, which had become my saving grace. I loved punching the heavy bag, venting all my frustration, and I so enjoyed seeing my body develop and my muscles getting bigger. I was religious about taking vitamins and drinking protein shakes, and I'd wake up every morning already looking forward to that day's workout. I started buying books on bodybuilding, and where most kids' idols were NFL or Major League Baseball players, mine came from the likes of Lou Ferrigno and Arnold Schwarzenegger. All I wanted was to get back to the grind, although I hadn't really figured out what that grind would be like in my new reality.

And there was another plus side. My mother had always wanted a pool, and my situation was ultimately what led to my father finally caving and installing one on the pretext that it would be "very good for Donald." And it was, but my father ended up being the one who enjoyed the pool more than any of us.

At some point I know we celebrated me turning seventeen, but I don't remember a party, a cake, or blowing out the candles. In fact, I don't remember anything about that day at all. What I do remember is how grateful my parents were for my high school sending my teachers, who were brothers and laypeople, over for the one-on-one sessions that kept me from having to repeat my junior year.

Thanks to the freedom provided by the prosthetic device acting as a cast, I also took to riding a stationary bike in the basement, which was actually easier than walking with a cane since it was so simple to position my foot on the pedal in a way that put no pressure on it. I became so fluid at it, I entered a local three-mile bike-a-thon that kicked off not far from my house. I rode my bike over that Saturday morning to join the other riders. I don't remember where in the pack I finished, but I *finished*.

And that was more than enough.

PART TWO

DO IT NOW

I expect to pass through this world but once.

Any good thing, therefore, that I can do or any kindness I can show to any fellow human being, let me do it now.

Let me not defer or neglect it, for I shall not pass this way again.

—Stephen Grellet

8

DIAGNOSIS

"The biopsy came back positive," my doctor told me from across his desk.

It wasn't a complete surprise; in fact, it wasn't a surprise at all. We'd scheduled the biopsy because of a spike in my PSA, or prostate-specific antigen, level and because of my family history. My older brother Ben had suffered from prostate cancer, and my father had died from it four years or so after he'd been diagnosed back when treatments weren't nearly as varied or effective.

This was 1999, and I was only thirty-seven years old, more than twenty years removed from my hunting accident. I remember going back to my general practitioner to review the results.

"Here's what I'm seeing," he said. "Your PSA is only two point six. You're within the range, which is good news."

The PSA test is measured on a scale between zero and four. And my doctor was right—normally, 2.6 was acceptable, though a bit high for a man my age, especially given my family history. So my doctor ordered a second test for later that month.

The result: 3.9. A terrific grade point average for a high school or college student but a lousy PSA level that strongly suggested I had prostate cancer. That's when I insisted on scheduling a biopsy to determine it one way or another. My brother had already been through this and became my guide, along with my wife, Deirdre, who was a registered nurse.

My brother referred me to a renowned prostate cancer surgeon named Herb Lepor, who had studied under the legendary Dr. Patrick Walsh from Johns Hopkins. Dr. Lepor listened carefully to what I was saying, took copious notes, and scheduled a biopsy. It's not a pleasant procedure. A technician goes in through your rectum with a wire and snips samples from several representative areas of the walnut-size prostate, in my case taking twelve samples. That's key, because the cancer could be growing in any number of places, and absent a diverse sampling, it's possible to get a false negative result.

Not only did the results of that biopsy confirm that I had cancer, but also according to the Gleason score on which prostate cancer is rated on a scale of one to ten, mine came in between seven and eight. Not good, because that indicated this was an especially virulent and aggressive form.

Dr. Lepor had an easygoing manner that I found very reassuring, hardly the boastful, aggressive type I'd expected from a man of his reputation in the field. He wore a white lab coat and spoke softly and directly. He projected confidence and reassurance in the case of a devastating diagnosis.

"We should discuss possible treatments," Dr. Lepor advised. "Review your options."

My general practitioner had originally deemed that I may have been overreacting by insisting on the PSA test and biopsy. His thinking was that otherwise healthy thirty-seven-year-old men don't contract prostate cancer, but my family history made me err on the side of caution, and that almost surely saved my life. That said, Dr. Lepor wanted to offer me alternatives outside of surgery—the side effects of radical prostate surgery were well established and even more dramatic for a man as young as I was.

I went to the appointment with Deirdre so she could cut to the chase of all the medical terminology. In any event, patients for this kind of meeting are strongly advised to bring a family member or other potential caregiver with them, and that paid off in a big way. As a nurse, she was processing the information much faster than I was. She listened carefully and weighed the choices of treatment from a clinical perspective, whereas all I was thinking was getting the cancer out of me as quickly as possible. My worldview has always been dominated by realism and pragmatism. As a builder, which is where I've spent the vast bulk of my professional career, if something goes wrong at a job site I'm running, I want to know about it, and I don't want the truth sugarcoated. I'm the kind of person who likes to deal with problems head-on, an inclination I share with my father; my feeling is nobody ever achieved success by sidestepping issues or viewing the world through rose-colored glasses. The fact that I had come prepared for the diagnosis helped inform my attitude.

For his part, Dr. Lepor seemed excited to have an opportunity to treat a prostate cancer patient as young as me. In addition to being a renowned surgeon, he was also on the medical faculty at New York University (NYU) Medical Center, and my case presented a unique teaching opportunity, since thirty-seven was so far below the normal age of the patients he ordinarily saw.

But that didn't change the fact that I was suffering from the same disease that had killed my father a dozen years earlier when he was seventy-four, and I spent a good portion of the rest of the week ruminating on just that. I was only twenty-five years old at the time my father died. My father was forty-nine when I was born, the age when many men are becoming grandfathers instead. My mother told me my birth wasn't planned, but I had been a nice surprise. That said, neither that nor my father's age was the reason for the distance that defined our relationship.

As I said, my dad was all business all the time, hardly the type to go outside and toss a football or baseball around, maybe shoot baskets in a driveway b-ball hoop. That just wasn't him. Instead, I had a brief window with him after church on Sundays when we'd do something together. I also remember a few times when he took me to the Central Park Zoo when it was still top-notch and featured a rare gorilla enclosure. That passed for bonding time, other than the work we'd put in at the laundry that was the proverbial family business.

My father saw putting me to work from a very young age as a way to instill in me a strong work ethic. I shifted sheets from one machine to another, moved hampers, folded towels, and swept up the floors. I actually kind of liked it, since it was the only time I really got to spend with my father. The fact that he was back in the office while I was on the floor didn't matter as much, since we were within yards of each other and I wanted to make him proud.

That said, I was always envious of my friends, all of whom had younger fathers and enjoyed quality time with them outside of working. They coached their sons' Little League baseball or PAL football teams. They took their families on trips and vacations. They went to the movies or out to dinner with their kids, just because they could. My father felt he always needed to be on the job. If the business was open and his employees were at work, then he had to be there too. Some would define him as a workaholic, but my dad just saw it as the right thing to do. He never turned the air-conditioning on in the front of the building, because the cleaning plant in the back didn't have any. And if the workers there were going to toil in the heat, then so would he and the rest of those who worked up front. My dad didn't discriminate. The men working up front would strip down to their undershirts, and the women's lipstick would literally melt in their handbags.

Similarly, my father was old-school in the sense that he rarely expressed much, if any, emotion. I never knew what he thought of me, because he was never one to even say "Good job!" much less "I love you." He was a part of a generation that didn't believe in superlatives, valued hard work for its own sake, and expected us to feel the same way as if it were baked into our genes. He never wanted to hear that any of us were going to work in anything other than the family business. That was a given for him, a reality he equated with an involuntary act like breathing. He wanted us to be the best we could be and genuinely believed hard work from a young age was the best way to go about that.

I'm not sure if he felt we owed it to him so much as he had built something he wanted to pass on to his children. That's a very worthwhile endeavor, but one that exchanged his thinking for our own. His priorities, in order, were work, church, and family, whereas mine are family, church, and work. That's not meant to criticize my father, though, because he came from the generation responsible for building the middle class and the country itself. Because of men like him creating and growing businesses like his, people could own a piece of the American Dream, starting with their own home. They could afford to send their kids to college, a decent car or two, and an annual family vacation, even if he never went on one himself. His duty was to a higher calling, most particularly his family.

"I took all the risk," he'd tell us, "so the rest of you don't need to take any more."

That moment helped crystallize in my mind why he'd never made time to toss a ball around with me: he was too busy building a business that could support his entire family. He wasn't about to hand us anything, but he had made sure the opportunity was there for us to grab if we wanted it. In that respect, he'd taken something from me in order to provide me with something else.

My father's philosophy could best be described as *life isn't fair—get used to it.* Suck it up, in other words. And if we did something wrong, in his mind it was because we didn't try hard enough.

I might never have known what he was thinking, but I never wanted to disappoint him. His approval meant everything to me, perhaps because he displayed it so rarely, but that only pushed me to do more and work harder. So I guess you could say my father also taught me determination and resolve. I never left a job poorly finished or unfinished, not so much because I feared his wrath as I continued to seek the approval I so rarely gained.

My father would say things like, "When you walk into the laundry to work, walk fast. Have a place to go, and be a mirror of what you want to be. And, most of all, don't ever ask someone to do what you wouldn't do yourself."

Because he died when I was so young, so many of my most dominant memories were of the last four years of his life after he was diagnosed with prostate cancer at the age of seventy, much too late for the treatments to be effective. He suffered through surgery and round after round of radiation that sapped his strength and, ultimately, left him too feeble to climb the stairs. We moved a hospital bed into the same family room where I had recovered from my hunting accident, but unlike me, my father wasn't going to recover.

I'll always remember the day my father died, January 27, 1986, because the space shuttle *Challenger* tragically blew up a day later, killing all seven astronauts on board. He died without drama or fanfare, surrounded by his family.

I remember the funeral home coming to get his body, I remember my mother crying, although the rest of us had become resigned to the inevitable and took solace in the practical reality that his suffering was over. I guess you could say, in that respect, he taught us well.

After my own diagnosis of prostate cancer, I took one final lesson he had imparted to heart. I had no intention of waiting too long to start treatment or to suffer a long, withering death as he had.

"I don't need to hear about other options," I told Dr. Lepor from across the desk before me. "I want the cancer out of me."

9

MY FATHER'S SON

Ever since my hunting accident, one of the overriding tenets of my life has been *just get it done.* Don't delay, don't put off, don't procrastinate, and don't drive yourself crazy reading reams of research that often prove contradictory. My informed decision, based largely on my wife's professional evaluation, to get the cancer out of me meant having my prostate surgically removed. No other treatment alternative promised the same success rate, especially because we'd caught the disease before it spread. My brother's research informed my decision-making as well.

In preparing for the surgery, it was hard to get my father out of my mind, how my early diagnosis was giving me a chance he never got. Right up until today, I think about how his style of parenting informed my approach to fatherhood and the relationship I have with my own four children. Fortunately, my children had all been born by the time of my diagnosis, since I obviously wouldn't be having any more. I had a daughter named Devon (who was five at the time) to go with my three sons, Patrick (two), Tim (seven), and Donald (nine). I was proud of them all and took special pride in the fact that each was their own person at such young ages, even

Patrick. They were too young to grasp what was going on, so we didn't bother explaining what they wouldn't understand anyway. My father had died before any of them were born, so they carried no particular recognition of the "C" word. I was fortunate in the fact that my wife and I had decided to have a family young. Four kids were enough for any man.

I'm a realist, and I attacked beating cancer the way I would any other challenge I faced. I was hardened about such things, given all I'd gone through in the wake of the hunting accident. If I could prove the doctors wrong about my ultimate prognosis then, I could beat cancer now.

I had often dwelled on the differences between my father and me. In that medical facility though, while waiting to see the doctor, I started to think about how we were more the same. These thoughts had likely been spurred by the fact I knew I was about to be diagnosed with the same disease that had killed him. His life, to a great extent, had been consumed by issues pertaining to his business. My life philosophy, in contrast to his, which was focused on business, can best be summed up as *enjoy your family*. I want my children to be open and honest with me, to tell me the truth about how they feel, especially when they disagree with me. Above everything else, though, I always tell them that I love them, something my father never said to me. And the only thing I might say to them more often than that is "good job." I want them to know I'm paying attention to what they're doing in their lives. I want them to feel comfortable coming to me about anything and everything.

Although we'd had time to process my father's impending death and prepare for it, the void after he was gone was profound. My whole life, because my father was so much older than those of my peers, I was always ahead of them in terms of life experiences, both work- and home-related. At twenty-five, they were losing their grandparents around the time I lost my father. I think that left me with a higher degree of maturity than they enjoyed, especially because I had gone through a life-altering experience in the hunting accident at such a young age.

That said, his death threw us all for a loop. My father had always been the glue that held everything altogether, especially from a business standpoint. He still ran and fretted over his business from his bed, and he treated his impending death as a business in itself and wanted to get us all up to speed so we'd be ready to step in when he was gone. Call that a seamless transition from life to death.

I never saw my father as a shrewd businessman or savvy investor, but it turned out he had actually excelled at being both. He was smart to buy up New York real estate. Once out of college in my early twenties, I oversaw an out-of-the-ground construction of a thirty-seven-story hotel with over two hundred suites, a $30 million-plus project, even though I had absolutely no idea what I was doing. That was of little concern to my father, because I was family, and he expected me to work as hard and as long as it took to master that niche of the construction industry.

My mentor, so to speak, at the time was a man named Sid Trout. His dad was my father's attorney, and Sid was the construction manager in charge of the crews and hiring of all the subcontractors. I learned early on that he was fine unless you crossed him, at which point he became truly nasty. Call it baptism by fire.

On another job I was overseeing that dealt with an extensive renovation, a resident came down and asked for help with a problem in her room. So, believing that we were in business to serve our customers, I sent a member of Sid's construction crew up to take care of the issue.

When Sid learned of what happened, he was livid.

"Who sent Bruno up to fix something on the sixth floor?" he demanded.

"I did," I told him.

"Where do you get off doing that?" he ranted. "Who the fuck do you think you are, pulling my men off the job?"

This all took place in the lobby, where Sid humiliated me in front of the entire staff, and here I was the owner's son.

I looked at him and said, "Sid, last time I looked, your name isn't on the checks."

His eyes widened with rage. "You know what? Fuck you, I'm done!"

And, with that, he stormed off the job.

This was a few years before my father died, so I called him and told him what had happened, expecting him to take my side, maybe even compliment me on how I'd handled the situation, because all I'd done was help a guest whose window blind had fallen off.

"What?" he said, in a calm and matter-of-fact manner that told me he knew I was right but still had to play the game. "Son, you need to eat crow."

"What are you talking about, Dad?"

"You have to go back to Sid and apologize."

Not only did I have to apologize, as it turned out, but Sid made me beg for his forgiveness. And over the course of months, he'd criticize many of my team members to me because he didn't think they were pulling their weight in the family business we had divided up to keep things running. Chances are, of course, he was badmouthing me to them at the same time. And we all kept quiet because we believed that Sid was the only one who could get the things that needed doing done. With my father gone, he had become even more important to the company and took advantage of the situation. Basically, he bullied us because he considered himself indispensable. I was quickly moving up the ranks, but I was still too young for anyone to believe I could do the job as well as Sid.

Sid would complete a minimal amount of rooms a year because he was so anal. He worked without a budget and was a weight on the family's business and my sanity. He would have our men redoing walls, for example, over and over again on our dime. He proceeded based on whim with no plans, no drawings. It wasn't coming out of his pocket, so what did he care? But we tolerated him because we didn't feel we had a choice.

Finally, it got to be too much, and my brother Ben let him go. Only after he was gone did we truly realize not only what a bad person he was, but also that he wasn't all that good at his job. This represented a crucial demarcation point for the family business, because it was now ours, ours to leave our mark on. We no longer needed to cower in fear of Sid or kowtow to his demands or his ego. We got rid of him and, in the process, put our stamp on a business that ultimately became a thriving boutique hotel brand under our ownership and management.

We were able to take what my dad had built to the next level. My father was astute enough to have acquired various buildings that specialized in what amounted to long-term stays, usually around a month in duration. When we took over, we saw the opportunity to move into a niche that would separate us from run-of-the-mill chain hotels as something special and unique, what's called "boutique" today. We all took roles that best suited our skill sets, mine eventually being the director in charge of construction and renovation, having already proven myself in that regard. We not only changed the business model, we started acquiring more properties that best conformed to the model we were creating. Prior to that, everything had been done by the seat of the pants, kind of an ad hoc process where things were made up as they went along. We took a more sophisticated, pragmatic approach.

My grandparents had started a dry-cleaning laundry business on 64th Street and Third Avenue in Manhattan. When the men went off to fight in World War II, the women of the family, under my grandmother, ran the business pretty much by themselves. My father never spoke much, if at all, about his experience in the war. I think I learned from one of my uncles that he had fought in the Battle of the Bulge. I only found his ribbons, medals, and commendations, including the Purple Heart, after his death, and they are now proudly displayed in my home. During the war, the women did such a great job stepping in for him and his brothers that they left them with a rock-solid foundation off which to build what started as modest real estate investments, laying a similar foundation for what we inherited and expanded. Because health issues prevented him from serving, my Uncle Dan stayed behind with his mother and her sisters, which proved vital because he was the most familiar with the day-to-day operation of the business.

Ultimately, our brand built on humble roots grew to a string of boutique hotels in New York City. Building his real estate portfolio had required my father to take so many risks and accumulate so much debt that he had flirted with financial disaster during the economic downturn of the 1970s. But he had stuck it out and weathered the storm as he always did, until he ran into the one opponent he couldn't beat in prostate cancer.

And now I was facing that same enemy.

10

CUTS LIKE A KNIFE

At thirty-seven, I was half my father's age when I was diagnosed. I had watched him wither and die from the side of his hospital bed in our family room. I'd witnessed him suffer through all the radiation treatments in the hope it would slow the cancer's spread and buy him some more time.

Although the current state-of-the-art robotic surgery was not in fashion yet, Dr. Lepor had mastered the nerve-sparing technique championed by his mentor, Dr. Patrick Walsh, that allowed for surgical removal of the prostate with less severe side effects than the previous surgical treatment. Even so, I was warned that I might be impotent and incontinent for the rest of my life, just like twenty years before when doctors told me I'd never walk on my own two feet again.

Here I go again, I thought.

Only this time, the doctors were far more likely to be right.

The surgery, which happened right before Christmas of 1999, went extremely well. My wife accompanied me to the New York University Medical Center, our two older kids were in school, and my wife's parents were watching our youngest two, Patrick and Devon. My brother Ben joined Deirdre and her brother Brian in the waiting room through the duration of my surgery. In all, ridding my body of the scourge that had killed my father took maybe two hours, and I was released from the hospital with a catheter inserted into my urethra and a bag fastened to my leg to collect the urine draining out of my bladder.

Unfortunately, the side effects I'd hoped would be mild and temporary proved to be anything but, at least initially. Sure, I'd been warned about incontinence and impotence, but I found the effects of the former to be profoundly unsettling, psychologically as much as anything. Our youngest son was still in diapers at the time, and here was my wife buying diapers in one aisle and Depends for men in the other. Deirdre was the real trouper through the entire ordeal, changing the urine bag that was clipped to my leg. She assumed the role of a nurse rather than a wife and treated me like a patient instead of a husband. The ordeal drew us closer, while other couples we knew were starting to grow apart.

Even as my symptoms began to abate, I wanted to help others by testing out experimental treatments for impotence that might relieve those life-altering side effects, and willingly became a human guinea pig so other men could be better informed about their post-surgical options. I tried several medications but quickly abandoned them of the side effects. I had to travel a lot at the time, because I was scouting out new real estate properties to potentially acquire. I carried a briefcase with me so every night without fail I could hook up nodes to my privates at night in the hope that electrical stimulation would offer at least a measure of function. Because I was so young, I was willing to try anything that would help others stricken by this disease and were facing the same future I was live a normal life.

As for the incontinence I suffered, I donned diapers for a couple of weeks until the indignity of their use led me to stop using them, just as I had shed the prosthetic cast fashioned for me after the hunting accident. That didn't change the fact that the surgery had left me unable to hold urine in my bladder, so whenever I drove I carried an empty bottle with me. When I had to go, I had to go. Period. Surgery had robbed me of the ability to hold the flow off by clenching. Still, I was determined to beat the record for shortest duration with a catheter among Dr. Lepor's hundreds of patients, which was ten days at the time. I beat it by three days. Removal occurred in the operating room suite he maintained in his actual office. A nurse instructed me to lie down on a cold steel table.

"You may feel a twinge of pain," she warned, beginning to pull.

Twinge? It was agonizing, and the process took so long I thought the catheter must have been a hundred feet long.

In Dr. Walsh's book on prostate cancer, considered the definitive study on the subject at the time, he also delved into the effects prostate cancer has on spouses, who often suffer more than the actual patients, their husbands. Unbeknownst to me, my wife and mother of our four young children was also processing the idea of becoming a widow, a single mother of four at the age of thirty-six. She only told me about this years later, as she never wanted to add to my plight.

Fortunately, as a nurse, she understood going in what both of us would be facing. Her enviable attitude could best be summed up as we were in this together and that's the way we would deal with it. I was eventually able to get an erection again, but without a prostate I could no longer ejaculate, which left me feeling as if my manhood was gone.

Of course, the notion of manhood is open to interpretation. It's in your head, as well as your groin. But what makes a man? I was still a father, a husband, a businessman. None of that had changed, something I reminded myself of constantly. I had produced a wonderful family, and they were no less that in the face of what I had lost. And I genuinely believe I've become a better man and a better father thanks to these things I had so long taken for granted.

As a woman and a nurse, my wife understood all too well what mastectomies performed on women suffering from breast cancer can do to their psyche and self-image. Too many consider their womanhood to be gone in the wake of such disfigurement that leaves them no longer feeling whole. My side effects, while uncomfortable and unnerving, had not altered my physical appearance, so I could go anywhere and do anything, secure in my manhood, so long as I brought along one of those bottles for the ride, since my urgency to go remained that much more pronounced.

The best results I got at the time for impotence were from a therapy that included an injection that produced a lasting erection that helped me retrain my body and mind. The problem was the erection lasted too long, was incredibly painful, and required a second injection to bring back down. It was almost comical in a way and, I guess, sometimes you have to laugh. In my case, though, I told the doctors I'd share my experiences with any patient who needed my help. It's hard enough to talk about such issues period, unless you're talking to someone who's been where you now find yourself. I'm not sure I would have taken that opportunity had I been offered it, but I knew I wanted to offer it to others.

I find myself frustrated by men who have a history of prostate cancer in their family but still fail to get tested. They'll tell me their father and grandfather both died of it, and I ask them what their PSA is.

"I don't know" is the answer I usually get.

Then I ask them their cholesterol level, which pretty much all of them know. I find this even more frustrating now that Congress has passed the PSA Screening for HIM Act in March 2023, which assured that insurance would cover the test that remains the best early warning system for prostate cancer. The thinking, irrational in my mind, has been that prostate cancer is a disease you die with, not from. Try telling that to the men who are dying from it.

I took a businesslike approach to my cancer, and I was still working. Before we parted ways, I remember approaching Sid Trout.

"Sid," I said to him, "do you think the men respect you?"

"Well, yeah."

"No, you're wrong. They don't respect you, they fear you."

"So that's good."

"No, it's not," I told him. "Fear means they're just going to do what you ask them to do while you're there. Respect means they'll do what they're asked to do out of duty and pride."

In comparison to Sid, who became more of a nemesis than a mentor, as a boss I seek to be encouraging and supportive, almost the way I strive to be as a father. There are times when you can't be the nice guy, but my default setting is to respect my employees the way I want them to respect me. I suppose I learned that from my father, who never asked a person to do anything he wouldn't do himself. I was always motivated to get someone to set goals for themselves and help instill in them a desire to get better at everything they did. I was demanding, but also fair. I wouldn't just tell them they were doing something wrong; I would advise them on how to do it better, more like a coach than a boss. The key is to develop an innate instinct of what someone needs to become more successful whatever their role is within the company.

There were times, though, where as a boss I had no choice other than to let someone go. If anything, I was too forgiving, too prone to doling out second chances. I think I remember every person I've ever fired, and it was never easy. The problem with being too forgiving, offering too many second chances, is that it sets a bad example for the employees who are working their asses off without taking any liberties.

By 2006, having worked in the business since I was very young, I was ready for another chapter in my life. I left our real estate group, stepping away to pursue my own ambitions. I wanted to build something on my own, from the ground up. Beyond that, everything was aligned at this time to make such a move. At forty-five, having survived cancer, I was at a stage in my life when I began to focus on the long-term future of my immediate family. I didn't want my kids to coast through their formative years, believing they were just going to slide into the family business. I wanted them to be independent and not reliant on what someone else had already built.

So I went from being a professional buyer of real estate to a seller, enabling me to pursue other opportunities in the real estate industry I maintained great affection for. It had been in my blood for a quarter-century by then, and I was able to apply my talents elsewhere, starting projects from absolute scratch and building from the ground up. This also freed my children to pursue their own dreams instead of adopting mine.

As tough as my father may have been, he was a champion of just that kind of individualism, as well as believing we're all the masters of our own destiny. I wholeheartedly believe, for all the distance between us, he'd be proud of me today. He knew that nothing lasts forever, that even life itself comes with an expiration date. And above all else, he was a businessman and would have been the first to shake my hand after I closed the deal to exit the hospitality business he had started in earnest.

My father always said, "Save your money, because no morning sun shines all day."

I had always followed that piece of advice to the letter, not realizing that before long I'd be forced to take its meaning literally.

PART THREE

DO IT ANYWAY

People are often unreasonable, illogical, and self-centered.
Forgive them anyway.

If you are kind, people may accuse you of selfish, ulterior motives.
Be kind anyway.

If you are successful, you will win some false friends
and some true enemies. Succeed anyway.

If you are honest and frank, people may cheat you.
Be honest and frank anyway.

What you spend years building, someone could destroy overnight.
Build anyway.

If you find serenity and happiness, they may be jealous.
Be happy anyway.

The good you do today, people will often forget tomorrow.
Do good anyway.

Give the world the best you have, and it may never be enough.
Give your best anyway.

You see, in the final analysis, it is between you and your God.
It was never between you and them anyway.

—Mother Teresa

11

TO THE VICTOR

Early in 2000, to celebrate my triumph over cancer, my wife sent me on a trip to Florida for a little rest and relaxation with my two brothers: Laurence and my older brother by ten years Ben. This would be a true Orvis-like experience, referencing the company whose brand is based on inspiring and empowering adventure. We spent a few days at a wonderful resort, where we learned to fly-fish. In my mind, there is no better venture after a life-altering experience than to throw yourself into something new to celebrate both a second chance and new beginning. We caught a flight to Miami, ate a few stone crabs at the famous restaurant Joe's, and then made a leisurely drive to the Keys.

While I was no stranger to fishing, boats, and the ocean, learning to fly-fish had always been on my bucket list, and I would be doing so here under the guidance of an Orvis-approved guide. I lauded the grace of the cast as much as I reveled in all the wonderful places where fly-caught fish could be landed. I always looked to learn more about boats, fish, and fishing, and the notion of crossing this particular item off my bucket list was better medicine than any doctor could have prescribed. With my two brothers in tow, I learned about tackle, casting, tying knots, baitfish, flies, and retrieving a fly. Traditional fishing is typically done with a heavy lure and/or a light line (the lure drags out the line), but fly-fishing is exactly the opposite. With fly-fishing, a heavy line presents a very light fly. Learning the new skills needed for fly-fishing fascinated and excited me, and I was all in from the get-go.

Fate played out perfectly on that trip, making it all the more special and celebratory. We chartered a boat as soon as the lessons ended to go after the bonefish I was now itching to catch. We cruised out into the Atlantic, in contrast to venturing in amid the mangroves for a stealthier approach in a smaller boat, and got very lucky right off the bat, thanks to happening upon a migratory group. Instead of our guide needing to do some poling and spotting, all we had to do was anchor up and drop the fly. There were literally thousands of them around us, meaning it wasn't hard for even first-time fly fishermen like ourselves to land a huge catch.

I spotted a bonefish and made a cast. The fish swam up and ate my fly, and I was tight to a monster twelve-pound bonefish hooked to a fly rod. Little did I know that I would hit a home run like that on my first at-bat. My approach was, and always has been, catch and release, including that one. Bonefish don't make for great eating, but they represent the top of the food chain when it comes to fly-fishing. But a mount of that fish, based on the measurements I took after I'd lifted him into the boat, hangs in my home office to memorialize that very special trip. It truly was the catch of a lifetime, though I didn't realize that at the time.

There's much more to a fly-fishing trip than simply the hunt and the catch. Most important to me is the opportunity to spend time with my family and friends, building the unique type of camaraderie that happens on any kind of fishing trip, thanks to being united in common purpose with others whose company you genuinely enjoy, while doing something you love to create lasting memories. Going to new places is also part of the attraction, and since I like to travel, a fishing trip with my family and friends makes for a natural fit.

Fishing tends to slow the world down, time passing in hours instead of minutes. That allows for insightful conversations among family and friends that cover a wide range of topics we wouldn't normally discuss at home. Creativity and spontaneity take over and we have fun, almost as if time doesn't just slow down, it takes us backward to our childhoods. On one trip we were looking to have some fun after dinner and ended up creating a bowling alley from empty beer bottles. Oranges and grapefruits were our bowling balls, and we played game after game under the light splayed from tiki torches.

I am well-suited to fly-fishing because it's a quiet sport that begets reflection. It resembles hunting in that stalking a fish inshore demands quiet and caution. Strategy and stealth are of prime importance, as is patience. Suddenly, you find yourself conscious of the world around you down to the smallest detail. The sights, the sounds, and the smells are all magnified by the kind of hyper-focus that the rudiments of fishing involve. It doesn't matter if I am pursuing a striped bass cruising the flats of Long Island, New York, or a bonefish heading out of a mangrove tangle in Mexico. Everything exists in a moment which feels frozen in time, no sight grander than that of the fish that is about to become yours. I find fly-fishing to be the purest form in that respect and fell in love with it from day one.

The second-best thing about fly-fishing is the amazing places you can visit and explore in pursuit of the sport, any number of them being isolated and remote destinations that are the opposite of the buzz and commotion of New York City. There are few cars and no public transportation vehicles like buses, subways, or taxis marring the scene, and you can drive for miles without spotting a traffic light. Some fishing refuges even have laws prohibiting the use of horns, and there are no billboards to be seen. You may see a cop on your tail for a traffic violation, but not with his lights flashing. Locals walk, ride bikes, or zip around on motor scooters. Internet connectivity is scarce at best, and the pace of life slows to the kind of crawl that makes you feel immortal. As an added bonus, the cultures in these specialty fishing haunts are so very different that it allows you to experience new and vibrant lifestyles, pieces of which will undoubtedly accompany you back home.

For me, Mexico fits all those specifications and then some. There, you can chase three different species of fish when fly-fishing. One is the stealthy bonefish that prowls the shallow water looking for shrimp. Another is the picky permit, the silver fish that are broader than they are deep and are always looking to feast on crabs. Permit are among the most difficult fish to catch on a fly, though tarpon, the "silver king," often jump multiple times while pulling out incredible amounts of line with every run.

The Florida Keys, meanwhile, make for an eclectic mix of cultures and attitudes. While heading south from the cosmopolitan city of Miami and driving down Route 1, you can follow your progress from the mile markers dotting the side of a road surrounded by turquoise waters and small islands where, if you're lucky, you may spot leaping dolphins, diving pelicans, and a host of fishing as well as dive boats from the car window. Each Key is different from the last, from the civilized Key Largo and Islamorada to the primitive Deer Key and the colorfully-off Key West. Catching bonefish, permit, and tarpon on the flats, or snook and redfish in the mangroves, is a complete blast. You aren't just communing with nature, free of the heavy boat traffic that roils the waters around Miami; you are seeing the world from inside it.

The challenge with the Florida Keys, though, is that they're overfished. The whole point of going to more exotic haunts in Mexico, Belize, and Honduras or even over in Africa is because the human and boat traffic is so much less. You have stretches of water all to yourself.

When it comes to organizing a fishing trip, groups have their own tastes and preferences. The chemistry of the folks going on the trip is an important consideration, but our group always found itself on the same page. In large part, that's because we focused on more than where and when to go, adding to the equation what kind of fish to target.

Take the trip planning I went through in 2011 for a 2012 trip, for example. I had recognized that time was speeding by and I wanted to do something about it, so the most important part of that trip was being accompanied by my oldest son. He was in college, which meant my opportunities to take such a trip with him were dwindling fast. An avid deep-sea fisherman himself, this would be the third consecutive spring break he'd spend with me on a fishing trip instead of with his college friends wreaking havoc. He really enjoyed going well offshore for the likes of billfish, tuna, swordfish, and mahi-mahi. But since I do a lot of that kind of fishing closer to home, on this trip I wanted to focus on bonefish. The integral part of our trip was to find a place that offered both kinds of fishing, which was no easy task. When an island was surrounded by hundreds of square miles of shallow-water flats, for instance, the access points to the deep water necessary for offshore species proved challenging. That meant for this trip, to maximize our experience together, I needed to be a bit more resourceful than usual.

Of course, decision-making gets more complicated when you are trying to accommodate an entire group. So keeping the interests of my son in mind, I needed to find a place where he could be just as happy with his experience as we were with ours. Back to the drawing board I went, enlisting the help of a few of the guys who had pelagic fishing experience to narrow down the options. To complicate matters, many of us had already been to several of the places that offered bonefish, permit, and offshore fishing, but we remained committed to adding a new venue to our mix.

After a lot of back and forth, we finally settled on the Bahamas. I liked the Bahamas, because it's hard not to smile when you can choose from any of the seven hundred islands. The weather is always warm, even in the winter. People dress comfortably, and a natural ease and rhythm hang in the air blessed by a constant breeze. The main towns are port towns, tucked away in mazes where all sorts of boats are tied up in the dock-finger slips, including luxury yachts with long foredecks, large parlors, and flying bridges wrapped in tinted windshields. There are also plenty of center-console work-boats, with fishing gear and buckets on display. The sleek offshore fishing boats, with their tandem outboards, meanwhile, are ready to spring into action, highly polished fishing machines forever in wait of their next charter. The masts of moored sailboats stand tall above the buildings, ready to catch the afternoon trade winds. And then there were the solitary flats skiffs, with poling platforms, skinny bows, and beamy sterns that can speed you through inches of water and sneak up to casting range of a pod of tailing bones.

The buildings in the Bahamas resemble a combination of Mardi Gras and an Easter parade. They are brightly colored and represent nearly every hue found in a rainbow that alights in the sky in the wake of a storm, including yellow, fuchsia, mango, coral, lemon and lime, seafoam green, and pink. Music is forever playing around these buildings, along with the squares, and the smell of suntan lotion hangs in the air, blown about by the whims of the breeze.

As a man who appreciates landscaping, when in the Bahamas I always notice the relaxed splendor of the shrubs and tropical flowers. From the majestic palm trees with their sharp leaves and coconuts to the beauty of the soft, bright flowers of coarse hibiscus shrubs, the variety is stunning, forming a kaleidoscope of color and a bounty of shapes that are a feast for the eyes. The trees native to the area are tall and adorned with yellow plumage at the top that makes them look like nature's lighthouses. And the tropical tree's bloom grows wider and more colorful the hotter the weather gets. Bougainvillea plants offer bursts of bright colors like pink, purple, red, or orange that shift lightly in the breeze, as if casting a gentle wave.

I asked one woman who was born in Marsh Harbour if she knew the species of an especially beautiful plant I couldn't identify. She didn't but within ten minutes had summoned a host of people to offer their knowledge. She was related to half of them and close with the other half.

The Bahamas boast great food, from fish like wahoo to grouper to snapper, and delicious fresh fruit. The salty air, soft breezes, and talcum powder–like white sand make it no wonder that some three hundred years ago, Nassau and Freeport were pirate strongholds. Using the islands as a base, ships flying the skull and crossbones picked off slow-moving Spanish galleons laden with South American gold and silver when they passed between the Bahamas and the Florida Straits, easy targets for these ruthless looters.

Harry, one of my fishing buddies, took the lead in finding the perfect island in the Bahamas and settled on Abaco. Abaco is located in the Northern Bahamas and is comprised of two main islands, Great Abaco and Little Abaco, which are surrounded by about a dozen smaller islands, the entire area having been a hot spot for serious fishermen for decades. All the great fishing areas meant there was no shortage of fishing lodges in Abaco. After careful review, Harry recommended a relatively new place called Bay Lodge, thanks to its location on the western edge of the island, conveniently close to the Marsh Harbour airport. There were also some four hundred square miles of flats to fish, a huge swath for even the most determined and committed of anglers, that allowed both me and my son to chase the fish that were our passion.

The Bay Lodge was small with only eight bedrooms, a pool, and a firepit that offered fantastic views of the sunset. And it didn't hurt that the lodge boasted an executive chef who specialized in preparing local fare cooked to perfection. The short run to excellent fishing was a by-product of the location. We settled on the month of March, specifically the dates landing right in the middle of my son's college spring break. No, the two of us wouldn't be fishing together, but we'd be doing everything else together. I didn't know how many more opportunities I'd get to bond with him as I had for the previous springs. He wouldn't get to party with his friends and other college students again this year, but I was determined to give him an experience he wouldn't soon forget, a lofty goal that was realized for all the wrong reasons.

We were excited to leave behind the cold, damp, and icy winter winds of the Northeast in mid-March 2012 and trade them for seventy-degree weather and brilliant sunlight. Feeling warm, soft sand between your toes, even for only a few days, can carry northerners like us through the remaining weeks of winter.

On one of our previous fishing trips in the Bahamas, we had a stopover for one night in Nassau, and seven of us were dropped off by the lodge van at a top-flight restaurant. After enjoying dinner and drinks, we ventured back outside to find a bigger, more luxurious vehicle waiting for us. Inside were three extremely attractive, well-dressed women who were clearly escorts. Just as clear was the fact we'd been set up for a good time that none of us married men were interested in. Perhaps sensing that, or maybe just preferring his youth and great looks, these three young women descended upon my son. We challenged their chosen lifestyles but ended up all chipping in a hundred bucks to give to them to make their night worthwhile, even though nothing had happened.

Another time my brothers and I were staying in a lodge that had individual bungalows, all of which had tin roofs. There was this couple staying in one, both doctors and very serious, who didn't appreciate our antics or boisterousness. So one night I filled a wheelbarrow with coconuts and the three of us proceeded to rattle that roof by throwing coconut after coconut, watching what followed through a window. It drove the couple inside crazy, which was exactly the point since they had driven us crazy by telling us to pipe down and temper our raucous bar visits. The couple never said a word, never reported the incident to management. But their last night at the lodge, those two doctors did the same thing to us!

To go on a trip like this, not only surrounded by good friends but also in the company of my oldest son, was a dream come true.

Before long, though, that dream would dissolve into a nightmare.

12

GONE FISHING

Historically speaking, March can be a transitional weather month for the Bahamas. It's about the time that the Gulf Stream begins to push farther north, and the winds change from their northerly direction to a southerly direction. Some trips offer bright, sunny days while others may be cloud-covered and rainy. Fishing is fishing, and while an angler can hedge his bets toward the weather, the action is never a sure thing.

The only sure thing was we intended to have a great time. We all pitched in to make this trip happen. A few of my more gear-oriented friends were going to bring along an incredible amount of fishing tackle to equip us for bonefish, permit, and offshore fishing. Another was bringing enough delicious food to feed an army. A third kicked in a wide variety of drinks and snacks. It was all coming together perfectly. Waiting for our departure date to arrive made me feel like a kid again, counting down the days until school ended.

When that day came at long last, we all arrived at the airport and climbed aboard. Our spirits were high, and the three-hour direct flight went by in a New York minute. We arrived at Marsh Harbour Airport, were whisked through customs, and were met in the terminal by one of the members from the lodge to drive us to our home for the week. We passed palm trees, sand, and emerald-colored water on our way to the lodge, just a sampling of what the week promised.

Bahamian bonefish lodges range from rustic fish camps to those with all the bells and whistles that typify five-star resorts. Bay Lodge had been rebuilt pretty much from the ground up after Hurricane Noel leveled it in 2009, so it had all the shine you'd expect in a brand-new venue. From the phenomenal western sunset views to the pool and the patio, we had plenty of room to spread out and enjoy ourselves. After our initial introductions, we sorted out our room arrangements, unpacked our gear, and got ready for a week of fantastic fishing.

The manager dampened our enthusiasm when he explained that several weather fronts had moved in, conspiring to create difficult fishing conditions. Without bright sun and calm winds, it could be incredibly challenging to spot cruising bonefish and permit, and casting could be difficult in a boat pitching in a choppy sea. From what he could tell, there were going to be a few breaks in the conditions, enough anyway so that we'd get in a few days of good fishing on beautiful waters like we'd seen on our drive from the airport. At the very least, the tough conditions meant there should be no shortage of fish.

There were a few die-hards in the group whose enthusiasm waned a bit, but not the bulk of us. We were there to have a good time, and if the weather or the fish didn't fully cooperate, we weren't going to let that dim the experience we had so fervently looked forward to. The first night, everyone was pretty tired from the trip, so we didn't stay up too late. Good thing too, since sunrise arrived in what seemed like no time at all, and at breakfast it was clear our excitement to get out onto the water trumped the lingering fatigue.

When we walked down the dock, we couldn't help but stop for a moment and stare at the flats boats. They were long and sleek, with gunwales maybe a foot off the water and big casting decks, small center consoles, and wide platforms in the stern. Most flats boats have poling platforms that are fiberglass boards perched on top of a shiny chrome scaffolding. The guides would fire up the big outboards and whisk us through channels, along the edges of deeper water, and through skinny flats until we reached an area that held fish. Once on site they would trim up the outboard, grab an incredibly long push pole, and climb atop the elevated platform. That vantage point allowed them to see the fish from a distance, and poling the boat enabled us to make a stealthy approach.

Here's some more Bonefishing 101 for you. You fish from the front of the boat, the bow, while the guide poles and spots from the stern, calling out targets by location. The bow represents the twelve on a clock. So, once the guide spots one, they'll call out the location by saying something like, "Fish moving left to right, forty feet, at one o'clock," which is slightly to your right. Three o'clock is directional code for off your right shoulder, nine o'clock means off your left shoulder, and six o'clock is directly behind you. That communication helped us to get into a casting rhythm and properly present our flies. Back home, some of us wade to fish, some of us fish out of drift boats, and some of us cruise out of the harbor in big, high-sided offshore boats. The flats boats and the teamwork that a guide brings to the effort adds even more excitement to what already promised to be a great experience.

There isn't much that trumps the enthusiasm of a group of fishermen heading out for their first day on the water, and we were no different. Anticipation, excitement, optimism, and a dash of bravado were all part of the mix. We climbed aboard our various boats with our respective guides, the gear, some drinks, and lunch. The weather was a bit cloudy and windy, but that had zero effect on our attitudes or our plans. Instead, we were focused on rising to the challenges before us and to have a whole heck of a lot of fun in the process. Our clothes might have been dampened, but our spirits were as bright as they could be.

As my son headed offshore to chase big-game fish, the sixteen-foot skiff in which I was riding steamed out to the flats at full throttle. There was a chop on the water, and the wind combined with the speed made for a sodden ride to the fishing grounds. One of the best parts of the Bay Lodge was its location—we didn't have to spend much time running out to our fishing spots, so the spotty weather was little more than an inconvenience. The skies looked threatening, so I didn't bother looking up at them. Between lighthearted jokes and general banter, we were going to have a good day regardless of the weather or the fishing conditions.

By lunchtime, my fishing partner for the day, myself, and our guide, making up a trio that was standard for a bonefish foray, were a bit worn out. When you're fishing in an area that is best suited to being able to spot fish with the naked eye, a cloudy, windy day is about as bad as it gets. It was impossible to see any of the fish until they were so close to the boat that it was next to impossible to get off a proper cast before they spooked and headed away. The wind caused the boat to rock quite a bit, and although I have spent a lifetime aboard pitching vessels, the design and construction of flats boat rendered them very sensitive to even the slightest amount of movement. Sometimes it was even difficult to stand. Combine the rocking with all the fly lines on the deck, and I must have resembled a bobblehead doll in my attempts to keep from standing on the line while firing off a cast. Wind to a fly fisherman is like a cross to a vampire, and we had plenty of wind on top of the obscured visibility. Sometimes the breeze pushed my line where the fish weren't, while other times it ruined my backcast. Overall, wind is always a part of the game, but when it blows as hard as it did on that morning, it tires and frustrates any angler regardless of his skill set. The only difficult part about fly-fishing on the ocean is that there is no refuge free of the wind, and that meant we'd just have to deal with it.

When we broke for lunch, I was having a great time regardless of the challenges—maybe, in fact, *because* of those challenges. I'd make jokes about botched casts or blown-out fish. I'd chide my fishing partner about not being able to see the fish. We all talked about our families and our lives, and although we were tired and hadn't hooked a single fish, no one had lost his edge, his excitement, or his enthusiasm for the trip.

The afternoon session was similar to the morning: sometimes the wind picked up and we'd have to duck our heads to avoid hooking ourselves with a fly, and other times the wind dropped off and our hopes soared. We figured that a break in the weather would turn on the fishing, like the flipping of some metaphysical switch, and that we'd start hooking bones. As fast as the skies cleared, though, they would darken again, dashing our hopes. We had very few legitimate shots at hooking fish, and by the day's end we were ready to put our disappointment behind us and head for the Bay Lodge bar.

Our day was tough, true, but it wasn't anything that a hot shower, some dry clothes, a drink and a great meal couldn't cure. Besides, we were excited to rejoin the rest of our group to hear how they did on their respective trips. I figured their tales of being at sea that day would pretty much mirror ours and hoped none of their spirits would be reduced by the day turning into a bit of a downer. So I resolved to make sure that everyone had a good evening. I made it my mission. When it comes to fishing, you can book a trip, you can book a guide, but you can't book your weather. Having a few cocktails by the firepit overlooking the flats was a fantastic end to the day. Then, by the second serving of conch fritters and another round of drinks, everyone's spirits had brightened considerably with an eye on a better day in the offing tomorrow.

In some places in the Bahamas, fishermen expect to eat conch, conch, and more conch. While I enjoy sampling food from the region, particularly when it is served fresh daily, the chef at the lodge knew his way around the kitchen, creating masterpieces of ocean-to-the-table fare. Fresh grouper, mahi-mahi, and snapper were welcome additions to the typical Bahamian conch. Local fruits like lemons and limes were used in everything from cocktails to seasonings for fish and for desserts. A key lime pie, for instance, just somehow tastes a little different when you pick the fruit from a tree that very day.

Most of our group enjoys wine, and like kids swapping Halloween candy, we had all brought ample amounts of our favorites to sample while on the island. As it turned out we had enough varieties to hold wine tastings every night, and we worked with the chef to pair them appropriately to each meal. We all, of course, loved fresh fish, but to round out our menu we also brought in a variety of cuts of beef that rivaled our selection of wines in terms of quality. The weather that day may have disappointed, but we more than made up for that with a dinner extravaganza accompanied by an unparalleled spirit of camaraderie.

The coral firepit overlooked a gorgeous bay. As the sun faded away, the tiki torches cast dazzling shadows. Combined with the warm, salty breeze, we had the perfect setting for fish stories from other trips, jokes, and serious conversations about business and life in general. On trips such as this, we all ventured far beyond the routine of the regular world and dug just a little bit deeper into life itself. These were the kind of conversations that could take place only in a setting like this, our worldly cares and concerns left hundreds of miles away. After a restful night's sleep, the false dawn would light the sky, and our next day would begin with all the vim and vigor promised by the evening.

Mornings never come too early on a fishing trip, and I was up before my alarm sounded at 6:30. The typical morning was breakfast at 7:00 a.m., with the boats setting out to sea ninety minutes later. At breakfast we would decide on our daily rotation. Over the years I've found that daily rotation to be vital to the success of the trip. For one thing, we always rotated partners so that each of us could fish together on at least one day of the trip. It was a science of sorts, and based on the way the week was going we could pair anglers based on a number of factors. Sometimes, two fishermen want to target a particular species like a permit or a tarpon or a bone, and when they're on the same boat that creates a natural chemistry. Other times, some fishermen want to stay inshore and fly-fish while others want to head offshore and use conventional tackle. Where it really got interesting was when we created a pair that boasted two entirely different styles of fishing. Sparks were known to fly when we did that, and the result was some of the funniest post-fishing stories you'd ever hear. Grab a drink, pull up a chair, and plan on belly laughing until your sides ache—all in the name of fun.

We also rotated our guides. Every fish camp maintains a stable of guides who cater to different fishing styles. Some are patient and pole their boats slowly. Their keen eyesight covers every flat in search of cruising, mudding, or tailing fish. Those guides tended to be quiet, and they concentrated all day, right up until the boat was tied back up to the dock. Others were very energetic, bringing levity to the boat, and when they spot a pod of bones they exude as much excitement as their charter. Their exuberance for life overflowed atop the water, spreading to their passengers almost as if it was contagious. Guides also had particular areas they liked to fish and ways they liked to fish them, so by rotating the guides along with the members of the group, the overall experience would be both immersive and total.

Unfortunately, the second day of fishing mirrored the first. There were a few fish around, tough to spot and therefore tough to catch. The front that had moved in just before we arrived had stalled, leaving us with the same low-hanging clouds, gray skies, lots of wind, a chop on the water, and occasional cloud bursts of torrential rain that soaked us to the bone.

Anyone who goes on an outdoors vacation knows that, when it comes to the weather, we can do nothing but hope. And when things don't go our way, we grin and bear it, making the best we can of the situation. Days framed by perfect weather and big fish that were ours for the taking were akin to a skier encountering untouched, fresh powder or a golfer watching a drive sail down the fairway with the wind at his back. Absent that, we are left to make the most of what we have to work with.

While this is a challenging sport, it wasn't a competition about who among us could catch the most fish. The reason you release the bone from your hook and place it back in the water is to preserve a healthy population, so someone else can have the experience of catching and releasing it. And you're also preserving the way the multitude of guides in this region make their living. We weren't making a meal of our catch either. That's in direct contrast to the kind of deep sea fishing my son was doing. When you fly-fish, you can end the day without a single catch and still have a wonderful experience.

The stalled front created an effect akin to the movie *Groundhog Day*, every day taking on the same look, feel, and disappointment. By the fourth day, we had only a few hookups to show for our efforts, and the conditions were beginning to take their toll in the form of diminishing enthusiasm. Even a hot shower, dry clothes, and a wine sampling by the firepit failed to lift our spirits anymore.

I tried my best to keep everyone upbeat and did everything I could to chase away the glumness that was settling in. Every night I asked the chef to come out and do a presentation of our upcoming meal. He brought a much-needed lighthearted attitude to the group, and as time went on his presentations took on a quality that might rival an off-Broadway production. Food always has a way of putting smiles on faces, at least until the next morning when the first glance outside revealed more of the same dismal weather.

13

HARD BARGAIN

With only a few days remaining, our prospects for an epic outing were dashed by more clouds, winds, rain, and few fish. We had fun at night, but there was an edge to the atmosphere at the lodge. Fishermen want to catch fish, and we'd traveled all the way to the Bahamas to do just that, but here we were with fewer than a dozen bones in total to our credit. Morale was low, and it was getting increasingly difficult to get fired up for each upcoming day that promised more of the same.

Our rotation was keeping things fresh, but what we really needed to salvage the trip was a kick-ass day of fishing. I had fished with most of the guides, and when I woke up on Wednesday morning, March 14, 2012, I was looking forward to fishing with my good friend Gene and a local guide named Alfred. Gene and I had been very close for a long time, having both worked and fished together. Even if the current trend continued and we caught little or nothing, we'd still have a lot of fun giving each other grief.

In that respect, the sport of fly-fishing is much like golf, and not just because they're both so dependent on the weather for the experience you're after. Beyond that, they're both precision sports.

With golf you need to be able to measure the distance between the ball and the pin and then get the ball into the tiny hole. Fly-fishing is also a precision sport, based on your ability to cast your line with just the right amount of force to get it to land in front of the fish and then anticipate the bone is going to bite your fly as you're stripping it back. And the ultimate goal is to have the least amount of cast to get the fish to bite.

At breakfast, we looked out the windows. It had been pouring rain and super windy just before first light, but that latest storm appeared to be letting up. Most of the other guys were chomping at the bit to get underway in this window of decent weather, but Gene and I decided to hold off for a while. We knew that the water would be roiled up and murky and that no sun was in the offing again today. Combined with the fact that we were both beat up and tired from the previous day's pounding, we stayed back for a bit to drink coffee and for me to teach Gene how to play backgammon. Being a numbers game, he picked it up very quickly and actually beat me in our second game. He's an old-school Irishman and he let me have it in his thickest Irish accent when he took me down.

"That'll teach ya!" Gene laughed, rubbing his hands together. "What do you say to another game?"

The wind was gusting, and whenever we looked up we'd see the water churning and white caps frothing. We sighed, poured another coffee, and went back to our game. At around ten that morning, the weather pattern began to turn. Evidently the front was finally passing through at long last. The winds calmed, and the gray skies were slowly replaced by pockets of bright sunshine, just the weather we had expected in the Bahamas and the very reason we were there. Gene and I abandoned our third game halfway through when the first rays of sunshine broke, and headed out to get our gear.

Our guide for the day, Alfred, had been hanging around the lodge waiting for us. We grabbed our rods, fly boxes, lunches, and rain gear and headed for the dock. Alfred fired up the outboard and pushed his skiff away from the dock, and in a few moments we were cruising out onto the bay at full throttle. Finally, a beautiful day that was perfect for fishing!

We hit a few spots, with Gene and I taking turns casting our rods. Although the weather had calmed, the clouds swiftly rolled back in, stealing the sun from us, and the seas were still pretty tough. The weeklong blow made a mess of things, and it would be a while before the water returned to its normal clarity. Sunshine would have made things a lot better, but at least we could see some fish, a welcome change from the other days we'd ventured out on the water. One of the coolest parts of fishing for bonefish is to see them tail. Their mouths are at the bottom of their face, so when they suck shrimp or crabs off the bottom, the tips of their tails stick out of the water. Seeing tailing fish gives anglers a clear view of where the fish are and which direction they are going. The tails we saw that morning were the first of the entire week, definitely cause for excitement.

The rough, cloudy water made the bonefish very skittish, so our excitement was short-lived. Because the storm had driven the fish off the flats, there were very few tails sticking out of the water. Conditions weren't going to return to normal for a few days when big schools of bones would gather to feed on the flats again and lucky flyrodders arriving at the lodge would be in for a real treat after we departed the island. Just thinking about that made our spirits sink again, so we stopped fishing and sat down to figure out our next steps.

Part of me was ready to call it a trip. It had been a difficult few days, but when it comes to fishing, weather was very much the luck of the draw. On past trips, we'd been lucky enough to enjoy perfect weather, perfect seas, and perfect fishing. This week had been the polar opposite of that, so maybe, Gene and I thought, we should just call it a wrap and head back in. Maybe spend the next few days lounging around and relaxing instead of waiting for the kind of conditions that just weren't in the cards.

Then Alfred offered reason not to call it a day just yet, telling us about one of his favorite fishing spots.

"Moore's Island is a magical place, mon. It is a small island, not far from here. Bonefish all over de place. Little elephants. Dey are little gray elephants. Huge fish, mon, and huge schools. Der's some permit too, but mostly bones all over huge, white sand flats. On a rough day you can see 'em and on a calm day you see so many your knees get weak. I bet der is some big schools down der right now. Tails tippin' up, dem bones eating shrimp like dey is goin' out a style. Wish we were der right now. Moore's is in de lee, probably calm down der too. Might see a tarpon."

Alfred had definitely given us something to think about, offering an opportunity we weren't getting here. It would have been easy to pass it off and just head in, but we'd come down here to fish and this might be our last chance. Of course, had I known Moore's Island was thirty-plus miles away, I would have said no fucking way.

"Well, no time like the present, I tell ya," Gene said, in his distinct Irish tone. "Let's go!"

Within seconds, Alfred's pole was stored, all gear was locked down for the long run, and we were underway. Even though we were in a fast skiff, it would still take us about two hours to get to the new fishing grounds.

Speeding over the water gave us a break from standing on the bouncing boat. We settled into the skiff's hard cushioned seats and held on tightly as the bow pounded through the choppy waves.

After an hour and a half of bouncing around in the seas, Gene and I had enough. It was windy, and every time the bow of the boat came off a wave, the salt spray and water soaked us to the bone. Rain followed the clouds, and the skies opened up. I had fortunately packed an extra rain jacket, which I gave to Gene.

In the Bahamas, it can pour so hard you literally can't see a thing. One guide at another lodge used to wear ski goggles during those cloud bursts. If we were near some mangroves or any kind of structure, I would have recommended pulling in and waiting until the deluge let up, but there was no land in sight. We were in the middle of the ocean with nowhere to turn, and in that moment I realized we'd made a bad mistake by venturing this far out into the deeper water, where the waves stacked up higher than in the shallows. The depth dropped from two feet to eight feet and then again to twenty-five feet and continued to deepen into the hundreds in no time.

"How much farther, Alfred?" I asked, amid all the bouncing.

He scratched his head. His boat had a broken compass, and with the limited visibility he had a hard time getting a bead on exactly where we were.

"I don't know, mon," he said, clear unease creeping into his voice.

"I wonder if we can get a signal out here," Gene said, pulling out his iPhone.

He hit the GPS, and sure enough, it worked! According to his GPS we had overshot Moore's Island, hadn't seen it through the cascade of rain blowing into us. We came about and adjusted our heading.

"Hey, Gene," I said. "Maybe we should rent a small plane for the ride back."

"What are you, a pansy all of a sudden?"

"Not at all, my friend, but that was quite a pounding. And I know from years of boating that a small, light skiff like this isn't meant for three-foot seas."

"Like I said, you're a pansy."

Gene continued to watch his GPS, directing us according to the coordinates it displayed. Sometimes the signal dropped and we tried to hold the course as best as we could until his phone reconnected.

"There it is!" I yelled, spotting a small landmass that had come within sight.

Moore's Island was in the distance, growing in scope just as the rain let up and the sun popped out. There were a few streaks of blue sky, and the wind subsided too. It was turning out to be just as Alfred said, and the reduced wind quieted the seas. The waves' peaks and troughs flattened out and suddenly, it seemed, we were in for the special experience we'd craved and now desperately needed to salvage the trip. By all indications, Alfred had been right: Moore's Island was indeed a magical place.

Alfred backed off the throttle as we approached the island. We puttered past a series of brightly colored homes adorning the shore, their vibrant hues welcome after the drab gray world we'd just emerged from. When the sun hit them, they resembled a rainbow.

"I'm hungry," Gene said as we approached the quaint fishing village situated smack in the middle of the ocean. "How about a hot meal to take the chill off?"

"I know just the place," said Alfred.

It turned out we were motoring into the capital of Moore's Island, Hard Bargain, an oddly appropriate name given how hard the last few days had been on the water. It also turned out to be prophetic in the sense of what was coming next.

We motored up to a structure on stilts that I took at first for a restaurant but quickly realized was a private residence.

"Alfred," I said, "this is somebody's house."

"Yeah, mon. Good friends and good food. Everybody welcome."

As we edged closer, I noticed there were a few fishermen in boats, hunting for stone crabs and spiny lobster. One fisherman stood in a long fiberglass workboat that was filled to the brim with his catch. Just looking at those piles of spiny lobsters and stone crabs that climbed so high it was hard to spot the fisherman's head made me ravenous. Definitely a sign for optimism, once we set back out.

"We'll have to grab some of those before we go," I said. "We'll surprise all of the guys back at the lodge with a feast of fresh lobster tails. Maybe we'll grill a few steaks too. It'll be the perfect way to end the day."

"Them stone crabs are good too," said Alfred. "Real good, mon."

"Good stuff," I said. "We'll grab some after lunch. The boys at the lodge will be in heaven!"

Alfred nosed the bow of the boat toward the building, and I saw there was no dock attached to the stilt house.

"Alfred," I said, "how are we supposed to get in?"

He put the engine in neutral, tied the skiff down to a cleat hammered into the building, and pointed to the rear window.

"You'll have to climb in through dat window," he said.

Gene and I laughed.

"Come again?" I said.

"You have to climb in through dat window."

"What are you talking about? You mean that in order to get into the house we have to climb in through the window? We can't just walk through the front door?"

"No, mon," he said. "This the only way inside."

I looked at Gene and shrugged my shoulders. We'd made grand entrances and exits in our day, but nothing even close to this one. And the sight of those lobsters piled so high had left me so hungry, I wasn't going to let such a minor impediment stop me.

"Gene, we're gonna make history on this one," I said. "You wait and see."

"Yeah, yeah," Gene said, "but will you get going already? I'm cold, wet, and starving!"

With nothing to tie the boat off to, Alfred left the motor running and held it in position while I walked up to the bow and looked up to the window I wasn't even sure I could reach. I rose up, putting all the weight on my right foot, and sprung up. I just managed to grab the sill and pulled myself through the narrow opening, landing on the wet floor that the lady was in the process of mopping. I looked up and saw her young son break out into laughter at my literal dropping in. Then I helped Gene in through the window, while Alfred motored off to tie the boat down to what passed for a marina.

"No one is ever going to believe this," I said. "You can't make it up!"

Gene wasn't listening; he was too busy looking for something to eat.

Alfred was right about the woman inside the stilt house—most restaurants in the remote reaches of the Bahamas don't offer as wide a selection as what we were treated to. We ate baked beans, some rice, and grilled chicken and ribs. It was as good a meal as I've ever eaten, in part due to the beating we took in the rough seas and the cold, wet day.

Afterward I felt more like taking a nap rather than going back out on the boat. But we had some business to conduct prior to departing with these fishermen who sold their catch directly out of the back of their boat. We met a local preacher, Reverend Simms, who was taken by my rain jacket because it boasted the name of its brand on the lapel: SIMMS.

"I'd give it to you right now, Reverend," I said to him, "but I might need it for the trip back. So here's what I'm going to do: give me your address, and I'll send you a jacket just like it as soon as I get home."

Reverend Simms did just that and then introduced us to the fishermen who were selling their catch right out of the boat. Thinking of our friends back at Bay Lodge, we asked for twenty spiny lobsters and about twenty pounds of stone crab.

"How much do we owe you?" I asked the head fisherman.

"Two hundred dollar!" he pronounced.

"What?" I said, flabbergasted.

"Okay, a hundred and fifty dollar!"

I realized he thought I was bargaining with him when, in fact, I'd been reacting to the absurdly low price. "How much do you have on you?" I asked Gene.

He produced around $500 from the pocket of his pants. Gene always carried wads of cash with him wherever he went, even when venturing out onto the water.

"Here," I said, handing it to the head fisherman in return for a festive haul to bring back to the lodge.

The man's eyes practically bulged out of his head when he counted the cash, smiling from ear to ear.

"Thank you, mon!" he said, clasping his hands in a prayer position. "Thank you!"

Similarly, I couldn't wait to see the guys' faces when we revealed the bounty we had brought for dinner. Meanwhile, the promise of decent weather in the land of baby elephants was more than enough to snap Gene and me back alert. We tucked our dinner haul in two coolers placed alongside one of the skiff's benches and set back out onto the sea.

The seas had quieted down and the sun peeked out enough for us to actually see fish. Fishing grounds around Abaco were a mix of white sand flats and mangrove edges, but Moore's Island was nothing but the most beautiful and expansive white sand flats I had ever seen. There were shallows for as far as I could see, with little bars and humps that were exposed at low tide. Channels surrounded some of them, and for a bonefish angler this was Valhalla.

Alfred poled slowly, very slowly, and pointed out ahead. "Bonefish, mon, lots of 'em, twelve o'clock. Look at 'em all!"

Gene and I stepped quietly on the bow casting platform, and before our eyes there were literally thousands of fish. I have seen big schools of bones in my life, but this one was off the charts. Here were fish for as far out as I could see, in every direction. As they moved in the current, more and more fish joined in. Some seemed to be coming from the deeper channels and the edges, and there was a seemingly endless supply of them. The little fish led the charge, and they were followed by medium-size fish and then by the true monsters. There were two-pound fish mixed in with five-pounders and then nine-pounders. There were even some that stretched into double digits in weight. As if that wasn't enough, the Holy Grail of saltwater fly-fishing, the permit, moved in as well.

It doesn't matter how many fish you've caught in your life, and I've caught a lot—a seasoned veteran who sees this quantity and quality of fish is going to feel like he won the lottery. We hadn't seen many fish all week, so spotting such a massive surge of them left us both awestruck and chomping at the bit to get back on the water to cast our lines.

A light rain started to fall, but we barely felt the drops. Gene grabbed his rod and stood on the deck while Alfred expertly poled the boat from the towering platform. He routinely called out casting positions to Gene, who did his best to comply.

"Bones at ten o'clock, forty feet away."

Gene turned to the port side of the boat, made a few backcasts, and stepped on his line during the presentation. The fly fell short, allowing no opportunity for a hookup.

"Bones at twelve o'clock, forty feet away. Get 'em, mon, get 'em!"

Gene cast his rod back and forth again, and this time he stepped in between the line and got it wrapped around his legs. I stepped forward to help him untangle the mess.

"Bones at two o'clock, twenty-five feet away. C'mon, mon, cast, cast, cast!"

Sometimes guides can push so hard you get nervous and stressed, and Alfred was clearly inside Gene's head. The more Alfred pushed, the worse Gene did. This time Gene hurried and created a massive amount of spaghetti. His line was knotted up, his leader was tangled, and I stepped in again to help him recover from the boondoggle in which he'd snared only himself.

"Gene, what are you doing?" I asked. "Get a grip! There are fish everywhere, all around the boat!"

"I see 'em, all right, but they don't like me much at all. I can tell."

A word about Gene. He is unusually determined, resourceful, a genius when it comes to numbers, and one of the physically strongest men I've ever known. Once he got out of his car at the top of a boat ramp on a frigid, icy day in South Hampton, New York, and left it in neutral, only to have the car begin to slide down the ramp atop the ice. So Gene literally planted himself in front of the hood in an attempt to stop it. The battle of car versus Gene ended up going the car's way, and he managed to leap behind the driver's seat just as it was cruising onto the ice. About twenty feet later, the ice began to crack, and Gene sank into frigid water eight feet deep. Even though he doesn't know how to swim, he maintained the presence of mind to wait for the car to reach the bottom, fill up with water, and pressurize before emerging and somehow finding his way to the surface, then paddled his way to shore with sodden clothes in thirty-degree water. That's Gene—resourceful and relentless. And then, soaking wet on a freezing day, he showed up at his job site to see how his men were doing. No one said even a word to him about his condition, as if this were normal behavior for their boss.

But it seemed today he'd met his match with his reel and rod.

"Gene, focus! Focus!" I advised him.

"I'm trying," he said. "If you think you can do better, you get up here!"

"No, I want you to catch a fish. Keep at it. But for God's sake, get the fly out!"

We went back and forth several times, with some casts being too far while others were too short.

"Gene, what the hell?"

Still other casts landed behind the fish or fell in the wrong direction.

"Are you kidding me, Gene?"

"Why don't you go fook yourself?"

Sometimes you just have to laugh, and I kept up the ribbing as Gene kept falling woefully short in his efforts. At least he'd beaten me at backgammon.

After a while, it was my turn. Alfred continued to move the boat to keep us on the pod of fish. He'd pole up into the wind, come about, and get the wind on the opposite side of our casting strokes. Fish continued to pour onto the flat, and turnabout being fair play, like Gene I went on a string of botched efforts.

"Not so easy," he chided, "is it?"

I wasn't tangling up, but I wasn't getting into the zone either. Finally, I calmed down enough to pick out a fish, relax, and lay out a good cast. My fly landed about six feet in front of it, and I leaned forward. Then I began the stripping process, when you're trying to entice the fish to eat the fly. You strip and then pause, because you're trying to get the fish to take what he thinks is his next meal. And if he doesn't take the fly right away, you continue the stripping process.

Strip, strip, strip . . .

Pause.

Strip . . .

Pause.

Strip . . .

The bonefish, a three- or four-pounder, raced up to the fly and looked at it. I held my breath while he seemed to contemplate the situation. Then I saw a puff of sand, and my fly disappeared.

14

CATCH OF THE DAY

He ate it!

I pulled hard to set the hook, and in an instant the fish was peeling off line in a mad dash. The rest of the school scattered, with some racing away while others closed in on my fish to see what was going on. The line was going out fast, and I jumped several times to keep from stepping on it and breaking the fish off. Fly fishermen hooked up on a fast fish look pretty funny, and after this week I must have looked hilarious. I didn't care. This was a good fish, and pretty soon I was into my backing.

Alfred moved the boat while I reeled in the line. Just as soon as I got the line back on the reel, the fish would turn and go racing out again. This beast wasn't tiring very easily, and he made three long runs. Fishermen live to hear their drags whine and their lines rip through the water, and this one did all of that. After the third long run, I got him to the boat.

It was my first fish of the week, and I was cranked up beyond belief.

Alfred unhooked the fish and rocked it gently in the current to revive it. Bonefish are silver and firm, all muscle, and at the end of the fight they are exhausted. He held the fish securely, placing his hand under the belly and moving it back and forth until its gill plates flapped open and shut. When it revived, Alfred released it back into the water to fight another day. It was strong now, and there were no sharks about that would try to run it down for an easy meal.

There is a distinct feeling that comes over an angler when a fish is released, and in a way it's like a good movie. There is a beginning where we are all supercharged to catch some fish. Then there is a dramatic rise in the tension when we either find fish or don't. That tension is heightened by finding fish and going through all the mechanics required to get off a good cast. The hookup and the fight are the climax, and when the fish is brought to the boat and properly released, the tension falls off, to be replaced by a euphoric sense of satisfaction. By the time I reached that point, when the credits would roll if this were a movie, I needed a break.

Gene got back on the deck while I sat down. For the first time I noticed that the clouds had rolled back in and the wind was picking up. It was raining softly, but I didn't care—I was used to it by now. I put my feet up on the casting platform and looked around. I had accomplished what I came here to do: catch fish. In contrast to the hard week we'd had, my feeling of contentment was overwhelming. I'd have a success story to tell when we got back to the lodge.

I thought about the other guys, and my son Donald too. I hoped they were finding fish in big schools as well. I looked at winning the battle against this tough bonefish as the turning point in our trip and that things would only improve from here. For now, though, we had more fishing to do, and it was Gene's turn.

Seeing a bonefish brought into the boat had a profound effect on Gene, and he wasn't about to try to one-up me after his first attempts had resulted in such a fiasco. His attention shifted around like the wind we were facing, and he set his sights elsewhere.

"I want to catch a permit," he said. "Can you imagine the shock on everyone's faces when we return? It's going to be great!"

There were permit in a wide variety of sizes ranging from small to very large. I think Gene wanted a monster, but at that point he'd have been equally satisfied with a small one. Alfred poled farther up the flat. The wind had kicked up another notch, and the rain had turned into a light mist. It cooled me off after the warm adrenaline rush I felt after battling my bonefish, but I didn't think Gene noticed the weather. He was scanning, looking through the water column in search of that telltale sickle-like dorsal fin of a permit. It didn't take long for us to find some, and Gene was ready.

"Permit, two o'clock, forty feet!" Alfred yelled.

"I see him!" Gene followed.

"Get him, Gene," I cried out, reenergized by the battle my friend was about to endure. "Get him!"

Gene was excited. Here was his opportunity, and he started his backcast. He worked out some line, then worked out some more, and worked out even more. When it came time for his final cast, it dropped down in an enormous bowl of tangles.

Ughhhhhhhh . . .

"Son of a bitch! What the heck am I doing wrong?!" he asked.

"Slow down and let your rod do the work," I told him. "Relax! Don't get into your head! Just relax!"

"Can't you see I'm doing that?"

"Well, relax some more!"

Gene tried a number of times on other fish, but he couldn't find any success. He was bummed and I knew it. I would usually give him a hard time, but this time was different. He was clearly disappointed, and I knew instinctively this was not the time to ride or razz him.

"Gene, I've got an idea," I said instead.

"I can't wait to hear this one," he blared, rolling his eyes. "I'm sure it's gonna be a good one, to make sure you come out looking fooking better!"

"Let's come back here tomorrow. There are a lot of permit around. We'll start fresh, and you'll get one then for sure."

Gene was quiet for a while. "That sounds like a good idea, all right. Let's get out of here. It's getting late, and I'm starting to get cold again."

It was around three-thirty in the afternoon, but the graying skies made it seem much later. We had a couple of hours to run back to the lodge, and if we wanted to get there in time for dinner we needed to move fast. The wind kicked up a notch, and I was not looking forward to the kind of pounding that we took on the way to Moore's Island. Both of us were pretty beat up already, and spending the next two hours in a choppy sea with falling rain didn't seem like fun. Add to that the mixed emotions in the boat: me being elated with my bonefish, Gene being bummed about his failure to catch a permit. Either way, our day on the flats was done.

"Let's call the lodge and let the guys know that we're on our way back and might be late," I suggested.

"Good idea," Gene agreed

"We'll tell them to push dinner out until we get back with our bounty," I followed, referring to all the stone crabs and lobster jammed into the coolers. "I can't wait to see the look on their faces!"

It was about four o'clock when I finally got through to the lodge. I told the manager we had a boatload of spiny lobsters and stone crab to bring back for dinner.

"Where'd you get the lobster and the crabs?" he asked.

"At Moore's Island. We picked them up after lunch. One of the fishing boats returned with a tremendous haul."

"You're *where*?"

"Moore's Island. Alfred put us on plenty of bones, and I got one and Gene had a bunch of shots at permit."

"What are you doing at Moore's Island? I thought you guys were fishing close to the lodge."

"We did," I said, "but we weren't seeing anything. There were a few fish here and there, but nothing to speak of. Alfred talked about Moore's and how great the fishing was, and we decided to go. No big deal—we'll be on our way back now and we will see you soon."

"Are you kidding me?" he said. "That's a long way away, and it's getting pretty stormy out there. Maybe I should come and get you. There is a ramp about an hour east of where you are. I could meet you there."

In that scenario, the manager would haul Alfred's skiff back to the lodge on a trailer, picking us up at around the halfway point. (As it turned out, the crisis we encountered happened well before that point, so taking him up on his offer wouldn't have mattered.)

"That's not for me to decide," I said. "Let me put Alfred on the phone, and you guys can figure it out."

I passed the phone to Alfred, and he and the manager chatted for a bit. I'm not exactly sure what they talked about, but when they finished Alfred cranked up the outboard, turned the bow of the boat toward the lodge, and pushed the throttle forward. We were off, on course straight for the lodge with no side trip to be picked up elsewhere.

Our positioning placed us on the lee side of Moore's Island, providing us with pretty smooth motoring on the flats. There was a slight chop coming from the combination of the wind and the tide, but not too bad. We were cruising quickly enough that the spray didn't hit us, so we were only soaked by the falling rain. I figured we would have an easier ride home than the trip out to Moore's, but that assessment proved wrong almost from the moment I'd formed it.

The part that you have to remember about the flats is that there are a series of depth lines you have to pass through in order to get to the skinny water. The first drop-off usually runs from the two- or three-foot depths to about eight feet. The second occurs a bit later and drops down to somewhere around 25 to 30 feet deep. The next drop-off is usually pretty significant and depends on the area.

Around Andros Island, the drop down to the Tongue of the Ocean is between 3,000 and 6,000 feet and is among the deepest areas in the tropics. Around Moore's Island, the depth drops to 350 feet and then again to nearly 800. Those depths aren't a lot compared to Andros Island, but they are significant enough indeed.

The issue for boaters is that when you move from the shallow water to the deeper depths, the waves increase exponentially. A slight chop on the flats turns into a two-foot chop at eight feet of depth. Our flats boat was ideal for the shallows but was absolutely the worst choice for a raging sea.

The sixteen-foot skiff pounded with every wave, and when the nose of the vessel came off the peak of the wave, it dug into the ocean and channeled gallons upon gallons of water into the cockpit. Alfred had to slow down but was still going fast enough for the water to drain out. I wished we were in a more seaworthy vessel, particularly one with higher gunwales and a closed cockpit so we would be insulated from the rain, wind, and seas. I cringed every time the bow lifted up, and I knew that when it came down the crash would hurt, rattling my spine. We went up and down like that for the better part of an hour.

Things got worse when we crossed over into the thirty-foot depth mark, where the seas doubled in size. The pounding became more intense, more water flooded the cockpit, and Alfred had to slow down even more. As if our trip wasn't rough enough, the wind speed increased and the heavens opened up in a torrential downpour. My muscles were sore, and every bone in my body began to ache. We simply had to hang on and hope that shallower water was up ahead, but after about an hour it seemed even deeper, and our anxiety was growing by the second. We were probably about halfway back to the Bay Lodge, but our progress was coming in fits and starts amid the wind and waves that were having their way with us.

I was hanging on for dear life and trying to focus on the water ahead of us for some sign of land. Because the wind whipped the surface to a froth and there were dark clouds and heavy rains, I couldn't see more than a hundred yards ahead. For all I knew we were headed in the wrong direction, but I did my best to vanquish that possibility from my thoughts. Instead, I just focused my attention on looking ahead and hoped that time would start to pass more quickly than it currently was.

A helpless feeling comes over you when you're on the water getting battered in a storm. You start to grasp the awesome power of the sea; how weak and feeble we are when measured against its whims. Our flats boat offered minimal protection at best, and I felt the first twinges of despair creep into my heart. I didn't know how much more I could take, and at that precise moment I stopped trying to think. Being subject to panic attacks, I knew I had to calm myself down, temper the fear. With no other options, I began to pray quietly to myself.

"Hail Mary, full of grace, the Lord is with thee," I started, looking to quiet the feeling of panic that was growing inside me.

After reciting the Hail Mary, I kept waiting for something to happen, and when it didn't, I just started over again.

"Hail Mary, full of grace, the Lord is with thee. Blessed art thou among women, and blessed is the fruit of thy womb, Jesus. Holy Mary, Mother of God, pray for us sinners now, and at the hour of our death. Amen."

Maybe I needed to pray harder or longer, both maybe, so I just began over again, and then another time. I couldn't help but recall clutching those rosary beads through my pants pocket after the shooting accident in the duck blind out on Cow's Bay as a boy.

Soon the praying quieted my frazzled nerves, and the ritual helped me find a sense of peace. I was no longer fearful but composed and at peace, in stark contrast to the way I'd felt before. I prayed that the wind would die down and the rain would disappear. I might not have felt as desperate as I had, but the rain and wind persisted, so I just kept at it.

When I completed my fifth Hail Mary, we ran out of gas.

15

BEACON OF HOPE

An unsettling quiet fell over our small boat when the engine cut out. The wind was honking, and it carried salt spray in the air whenever the boat cut through a wave. We had some momentum, but without the engine our forward progress came to a quick halt. The weight of the outboard was balanced with the three of us on board, so we remained in position for what seemed like an eternity. When the wind and the waves caught up with the boat, the bow spun around and we were positioned broadside to the waves before the reality of the situation hit us.

I was initially relieved that the pummeling subsided, at least for a bit. I figured that it would resume by the time Alfred switched the fuel lines over to the fresh tank he'd filled on Moore's Island, and then we'd get back underway for more crashing and pounding. I looked around the boat, but there wasn't an extra tank. Alfred must have stowed it somewhere.

"Where's the spare tank, Alfred?" I asked.

"It's empty," he said.

"What?" I said. "No, no! You've gotta be kidding me."

"No, mon," he said. "I'm not kidding. I forget to fill it back on Moore's."

I felt angry, resentful, pissed off beyond comprehension. I wanted to lash out at Alfred, wanted to scream and yell and shake my fists over such a display of incompetence. He was our guide. We trusted him with, above everything else, our safety. How could he have left Moore's Island without refilling the empty tank, leaving us to the crisis we now faced on the trip back? It was maddening, incomprehensible. In addition to that mistake, his compass was broken, he had forgotten to bring a satellite phone, and there were no flares or sounding devices on board, not to mention the fact that we were out of cell range. But I pounded only air with my fists, because what good would throwing the tantrum I felt inside me do? Certainly, it wouldn't improve our plight that was about to get further complicated by something else that was missing on board.

The boat was drifting and rocking hard from side to side. Every time it came off the crest of a wave we'd take on water, and it wouldn't be long before the cockpit was filled up. When we were motoring on the sea, the skiff drained consistently, but now that we weren't moving, our plight had grown that much more dire. The clock was ticking, and I didn't have time to do anything else but figure a way out.

I knew we'd have to set the anchor to keep from drifting back into the abyss of the sea. More importantly, we had to get the bow facing the wind so the cockpit wouldn't fill up with water as fast to buy ourselves all the time we could.

"Alfred, we've got to get that anchor set!"

I couldn't see him clearly through the storm, but his hesitation in responding was enough to tell me what was coming next.

"I don't have one, mon," he responded finally.

Again, I felt my blood boil, though not enough to chase away the chill I was feeling. Because of the small tides and shallow water, most Bahamian guides never need to make use of an anchor. If they're going to get out of the boat and wade for fish, they'll flip down the outboard and dig the skeg into the sand. But we had ventured far out into the open ocean, the three-foot flats a distant memory.

"Well," I said, fighting back the urge to lash out at him once more, "what have you got?"

"I don't know, mon. I'll check."

Alfred dodged around Gene and scurried up to the bow to throw the hatch open. I watched him push around some items, and after a moment he pulled out a grappling hook with no line attached.

"How about this?" he called to me.

In these conditions, a grappling hook was the equivalent of jumping out of an airplane with an umbrella instead of a parachute. But it was all we had.

"What about line? Do you have any line?"

Alfred went back to rummaging through the hatch and came out with a black polypropylene line maybe a bit over eight feet in length. Since we were in waters of twenty-five feet deep, it wasn't going to do us any good.

Again, though, it was all we had, so I set out to peel the layers away like a banana, thinning the line out while unfurling it to four times in length, to around thirty-two feet, which was more than enough to reach the bottom. Then Alfred knotted the remade line to the grappling hook and tossed it overboard like the makeshift anchor it had become.

I held my breath. The line stayed loose in his hands for a long time. The problem with polypropylene is that it floats. Normally, an anchor would be affixed to a chain, because the chain sinks to the bottom and allows the anchor to pull straight, keeping the boat horizonal to the bottom of the ocean. Fortunately, though, the makeshift line suddenly jerked tight. It had stretched out vertically, allowing the grappling hook to snare on the coral bottom and keep us from drifting. Right then the bow of the boat jerked around to face the current! I felt a wave of welcome relief surge through me. We were anchored up and had bought ourselves some time to figure out our next steps.

Finally, we'd gotten a break!

The rain kicked up and actually felt good on my face. It was cooling, refreshing, and I didn't mind it at all. I looked around at the way the wind was whipping up the surface, and for the first time since we ran out of gas I actually felt hopeful. I decided that I was going to look in the hatch, but my first step was surprisingly hard to take.

Because the cockpit was full of water.

We looked around for a bailer, and there wasn't one to be had. I remembered our sandwiches were in Tupperware containers, so I took them from the cooler and handed one to Alfred. Soon I heard scraping, which meant he had gotten most of the water out of the boat. I went back to the hatch to see what we could make use of from inside.

The sight was deflating; there wasn't much inside at all, practically nothing. There were four so-called "flotation devices." One was an orange horse-collar type that would fit a child, the second a white floating seat cushion with two fabric handles on the ends, a blue horse-collar vest with a CO_2 inflator, and finally, a black vest-style life jacket that looked to be child's size because, we'd figure out later, it was folded over and twisted. I handed that one, still the best one, to Gene because he couldn't swim, but he was only able to loop a single arm through it. The skiff's hard seat cushions did double duty as floatation devices, so we planted our backsides on them to keep us above the water that was collecting on the boat deck.

There wasn't a VHF radio on the skiff, so I looked for one in the hatch. Nothing. I looked for a first-aid kit, but there wasn't one of those either. I poked around in search of some of those space-age thermal blankets, and found not a one. I looked for an emergency kit or sounding device or any kind of pump—no luck. I checked my cell phone and Gene checked his; neither of us had a signal. All we had were spiny lobsters and stone crabs wedged into a pair of coolers.

Besides the Tupperware container Alfred had used to bail out the cockpit and the other matching containers tucked into the third cooler, that pretty much was the sum total of our inventory.

Gene was getting angrier by the minute. We looked everywhere for more items that might ease our plight but found only rusty hooks, lures, and lines—typical stuff aboard a skiff, none of which would be any use to us.

"Fooking great!" Gene managed, shaking his head.

He kept cursing, and I was trying not to lose my head and instead focus on what we needed to do in order to stay afloat and alive.

To be honest, my thoughts were a little jumbled. The true serious nature of this crisis was just sinking it. We were in dire straits. I didn't know what to do, so I opened the cooler, pulled out a couple of bottles of water, and handed one to Gene. We needed to start hydrating, because it seemed like we were in for a long night. Fortunately, neither of us had sampled any of the celebratory beers that were stuffed in the bottom of the cooler.

We were dressed for the tropics in lightweight fishing shirts and pants, Crocs, and rain gear. I had a skullcap and sun-proof gloves that retained little, if any, warmth in these conditions. I gave Gene my jacket to help keep the rain and wind from chilling him to the bone.

As fast as we bailed the water out of the cockpit with the Tupperware container, it filled back up. When the bow dropped down off the top of a wave, it dug into the sea and water poured back in. I realized we were sitting too far up and needed to move closer to midship to keep the boat balanced. I looked around for anything that would help us to stay warm, but there was nothing. All I could hear were the vicious wind gusts, and all I could feel was the driving rain that now felt like tiny needles pricking my skin. Add to that the shrill sound of the Tupperware plastic scraping against the fiberglass bottom of the boat. To this day, I can't get that sound out of my mind. It was not fingernails-on-a-chalkboard bad, but close, enough to make me grimace and grind my teeth through the whole process.

I sat on the white cushion while Gene sat on the orange horse-collar vest, keeping us out of the water that deepened around us, and providing some insulation from the cold, wet deck. Then Alfred got the idea to put the two coolers, filled with the spiny lobster and stone crabs, in front of us on the bow as a wind break. Soon we actually felt somewhat warmer and comfortable compared to the chill we'd been experiencing just moments before. We were keeping our bodies together to increase our shared warmth.

Sportsmen know that the time in the morning before the sun rises above the horizon is called a false dawn. In the time before the fiery ball shows its face, the temperature drops and a deep chill settles in the air. Once the sun climbs above the horizon, the light and the warmth are unparalleled, particularly if you've been out fishing in the pre-dawn hours. When the sun sets in the evening, by comparison, the effect produced is the polar opposite. The warm air gets replaced by a deep nighttime chill. The wind lessens before the sun drops, and then it picks up in biting fashion for the rest of the night. That was what was happening to us, and we were hardly outfitted to spend the whole night out there.

With the exception of a few patches of sun, we hadn't seen weather that was bright or light all week. And as we sat aboard the anchored skiff and watched the gray day fade to night, we realized that we were not going to be going home anytime soon. It had been a few hours since our last communication with the lodge, and they were probably expecting our return any minute. I wondered how long it would take before our absence led them to call the authorities, who'd never be able to locate us under cover of darkness in this slop anyway.

The wind started blowing toward what Alfred thought were the Pelican Keys. Alfred believed he recognized the cluster of islands by a red blinking light at the top of a tower. It was the first sign we had in hours that gave us the slightest inclination of our location, which gave me some hope, even though I hadn't seen the light for myself.

"That's Pelican over there, mon. I can swim to it and get help. It'll take a few hours, but I can do it, I know I can," Alfred offered. "I swam fourteen miles before with my daddy on my back once, and I can do it for sure, mon."

"That's a great idea!" Gene offered, his eyes lighting up at the flicker of hope. "Great fooking idea!"

No, it wasn't. You never leave the boat, ever, under any circumstance unless it's sinking.

"Good thought, Alfred, but we should all stay with the boat. It's safer that way."

"I can make it," he insisted. "It's not that far of a swim."

"Listen to him!" Gene implored me, turning back to Alfred. "Go, go, go!"

Alfred was ready in that moment to jump in the water. "I can do this!"

That's when I put my foot down. "I know you can, but we have more strength as a group. If we start splitting up, then things have the potential to get worse than they already are. And since it is nighttime, we've got a lot of other things to think about. We've got to find a way to make it through until tomorrow."

Though clearly disappointed, Alfred nodded. "If you say so, mon."

Somewhere around an hour later, he had another idea.

"What about the current?" Alfred asked us, breaking the silence that had settled over the boat. "The way da wind be blowing looks like it'll push us to Pelican Key. We lift da grappling hook off da bottom, and we'll get pushed right toward dose red blinking lights, mon." Again, he and later Gene claimed they'd spotted these lights, but I hadn't. "We keep bailing out da water we could reach land in a few hours. And if we're blown into shallows, then you two sit on da bow and I can pole us home. What you dink, mon?"

I thought that I couldn't even imagine us reaching waters shallow enough for him to pole. I looked around for Gene. He was keeping himself busy by bailing water with another one of the Tupperware containers. He'd fill it up, toss the water overboard, and begin again. Not only was this necessary, it was keeping him occupied instead of fixating on the dire nature of our plight, despite that screeching sound of plastic scraping against fiberglass that left me gnashing my teeth now instead of grinding them.

That made me think of Gene, wondering what it must have been like to be on a boat that was dead in the water and to not know how to swim. It was stormy, dark, and waves filled up the cockpit a little bit at a time. The driving rain hadn't let up in the slightest. The wind was constant, with big gusts interspersed with a steady howling that chilled us to the bone. Not knowing how to swim wasn't a big deal when you were in water shallower than your waist and the hot sun was beating down. But at night, in deep water when you were cold and soaking wet, it had to be downright terrifying.

I knew we needed to get him some relief fast. Alfred was right—if we could get into the shallows, we could pole back to the lodge. It'd be a long haul, might even take all night long for that matter, but if we were in skinny water and underway we would at least be doing something instead of just sitting out in the storm and the dark.

"Gene," I said, "we're going to lift the grappling hook."

"I heard you talking to Alfred," he said. "You think we're going to drift toward the beacon?"

Even though I hadn't seen that beacon, it had become, literally, a beacon of hope.

"That's our best shot right now," I conceded. "We'll lift the hook, and we'll see how it goes. We can take turns bailing to make sure we stay afloat."

"What have we got to lose? 'Sides our lives, of course," he added in a stale stab at humor.

"Pass me the container. I'll get the rest of the water out to give you a break."

Gene handed me the Tupperware, and I started tossing out the water. My hands were cold and wet, but we were almost ready to pull up the grappling hook. Anxious to get underway, I bailed faster and faster. Then, all of a sudden, a huge gust of wind blew the Tupperware container from my grasp. Just like that it was gone.

"What are you doing!" Gene yelled. "We need that to keep the water out!"

"It slipped," I said. "Sorry. Hand me another one. It's in the cooler."

"We only have two fooking left now. Don't lose this one too," he said angrily, venting his fear and frustration on me.

Finally, I managed to clear the water from the cockpit, and it was time to make our move. Alfred was on the bow getting ready to hoist the grappling hook, and for whatever reason, Gene started to yell. He started by taking the Lord's name in vain, and then he moved on to curse God and to rant about this being a perfect reason for why he hadn't gone to church in over thirty years. I hadn't seen this side of Gene before, a man willing to plant himself in front of a moving car to stop it from rolling out onto the frozen bay, but being on a stuck boat at sea in the midst of the dark and a storm without being able to swim more than explained it. It was clear Gene didn't notice that the more he cursed, the harder it rained.

"Gene, you need to cut out this bullshit and pray," I said.

And that's when I taught him to recite the Hail Mary prayer from start to finish, and we recited it together.

"Hail Mary, full of grace, the Lord is with thee. Blessed art thou among women, and blessed is the fruit of thy womb, Jesus. Holy Mary, Mother of God, pray for us sinners now, and at the hour of our death. Amen."

Then we began by praying for small things, like asking for the wind to let up and for the rain to lessen. We asked for the boat to be dry and for it not to rock so much. And we prayed when Alfred raised the grappling hook that we would be blown toward the flickering beacon on Pelican Key.

When the hook pulled free from the sand, though, the wind kicked up and there was a loud clap of thunder. The skies opened up and heat lightning started to flash in the distance.

In a very short time, low-lying clouds rolled in and our visibility diminished to the point where whatever beacon Alfred and Gene insisted they'd spotted was nowhere to be seen. The waters jacked up, and the boat spun around like a top until it settled in and we began to drift. We were moving, that was for sure, but the poor visibility made it hard to tell if we were moving in the right direction or being swept farther out to sea.

16

THE STORM

People who spend time on the water know that clouds will always point you in the direction of land. Clouds of any kind hover lower over land than they do over water. We couldn't see the red light, but we could see some clouds, and that told us that we were drifting parallel to land and heading toward where the light had last been spotted. I grabbed a seat cushion and placed it between my back and the deck for comfort, and then Gene and I huddled close together to stay warm. I began reciting the Hail Mary again, asking God to watch over us and protect us, and then I reached for my rosary beads but couldn't find them in my pocket. I had carried them with me every day of my life. I had them with me the morning of the hunting accident, I had them with me during my prostate cancer treatment, but I did not have them with me now, denying me the comfort they had provided on those occasions.

Some of our prayers were answered. The rain subsided and the clouds lifted so we could see the light on the tower on an island in the distance. All of a sudden there were other lights, lots of them, that could only be coming from what we hoped was Abaco Island, but it had to be a land mass regardless. We were drifting well now, faster and faster, and we had hope for the first time in a while. Gene pulled out his iPhone and, lo and behold, he had a signal! He pulled up a GPS map and for the first time in hours we could see where we were. He didn't have a cell signal, so I pulled out my phone and kept dialing the lodge. I dialed over and over again but after a while realized that there was no signal to get a connection.

Alfred took out his push pole and headed to the bow. One end of the pole featured a Y-shaped surface, triangular much like a yield sign that's open in the middle. When you're paddling with it, you're not really making much of a headway. Kind of like trying to mix paint with a toothpick.

But with every stroke the boat inched along. Renewed optimism filled us. It suddenly seemed possible, even likely, that we were going to reach the shallows and then the lodge in time for dinner. Gene's temper had settled down. He was studying his GPS—for what, I don't know, since he is technologically challenged.

After several minutes of careful study, Gene blurted out, "We're going the wrong fooking way!"

I didn't pay his statement any heed until he resumed even louder.

"We're running parallel to the cay, and from the looks of it we're heading back out to sea!"

Now I believed him. Gene tried to make a call but was no luckier finding a signal than I had been. I turned my phone back on and jogged it to the compass feature to follow our drift, and sure enough, Gene was right. We were drifting out to sea.

The boat continued to pick up speed as it was pushed by the current and wind. I told Alfred to toss out the grappling hook so we could regroup and determine our next steps. He pitched it over-board, but this time the boat's reaction was very different: it came about aggressively and snapped to attention abruptly, harshly. Then a wave hit us broadside. The bow started rising, and it was like a catapult. Alfred was pitched airborne, ejected from the boat as the cockpit filled with water.

Alfred had been flung out into the dark, choppy water. I kept my eyes on him as he disappeared underwater. As I waited for him to surface, I remembered he had told us he was an excellent swimmer. That better be true, I thought. Time slowed to a crawl, what seemed like an eternity really just a second. Then, out of nowhere, Alfred's head popped out of the water with his hat still in place. I turned away from him, back toward the boat.

The boat seesawed with the weight of the water, and we knew we needed to get it balanced quickly or risk capsizing. Gene and I fought to balance the boat against the rocking effect that was sending all that water swishing back and forth. First, we moved to the port side, then switched together to starboard, but it was no use. The boat succumbed to the weight of the water and flipped over on its port side in what I recall vividly in slow motion. Gene was pitched overboard, while Alfred continued to bob around on the surface.

I was being raised off the deck slowly by the flotation provided by the Crocs I was wearing. I didn't feel the deck anymore, and then I began to rise. I was tossed into the air like a rag doll. As I was falling, I found myself looking *up* at the hull. It seemed suspended for what felt like an eternity, and then it started to move past the upright position. I hit the water on my back with enough force to drive me under. My eyes were wide open, and the saltwater blurred my vision, but I could still see the shape of the boat as it continued to roll over on its port side. I remember one of my Crocs ending up floating away, while the other had somehow stayed in place.

Everything on board the vessel was gone, lost to the waters and the wind. Our boat had capsized. I heard Gene cry out and spotted him doing some version of the dog paddle that wouldn't stand up to the whipping currents that could drown him in a millisecond. The Styrofoam coolers we'd picked up on Moore's Island had broken apart, our bounty of lobsters and stone crab lost to the sea. All we had left within reach was a large Igloo cooler and a smaller Yeti one.

I grabbed the Igloo, worked my way up to Gene, and pushed the cooler up against him.

"Hold on to this! It will keep you afloat so we can work our way back to the boat!"

The way I saw it in the moment was that this and the other cooler could act as floatation devices. Along the way at one point, Gene let go of the cooler and almost sank.

"What are you doing!" I yelled out.

"My focking fingers hurt too much! I couldn't hold on anymore!"

"I don't care about your fingers. Grab hold again!"

But Gene couldn't reach the cooler; it had been swept away by the strong currents, leaving us with only the Yeti cooler left. Then our flats boat disappeared from view amid the pounding currents of rain, only to reappear moments later when the torrents and the wind backed off slightly.

Thanks to the Yeti cooler, we made it back to the boat with Alfred swimming just behind us. The capsized boat rose above the surface, like the hump of a whale. The three of us managed to loop our index fingers through the cleat on the bow to avoid sinking, while trying to absorb the shock of being capsized and regroup.

After a few minutes, Alfred eased his finger out, scurried like a spider to the bow, and clung to the side of the boat with only his head above the water. He had moved to the side of the capsized boat opposite where the waves were breaking, trying to find respite from the hypothermia we all knew would be setting in.

Alfred, a Seventh-Day Adventist, began to pray aloud, a long, rambling prayer. While I wanted to allow him time for this expression, an invocation of God's protection and mercy, I couldn't help but think that Gene and I wouldn't be able to cling to the cleat very long.

"Enough with that shit!" Gene said, panicking as Alfred finished. "We've got to try something else, I tell ya. This praying shit doesn't work. When are you going to realize that? It hasn't worked and it's not going to work. I'm not praying. If God answered prayers, we wouldn't be in this mess!"

"No, mon, you're wrong!"

"Start with an Our Father and a Hail Mary," I said. "You'll see."

"Not a chance."

"Gene, cut the shit. Let's pray."

"*Fook* praying!"

More Irish brogue F-bombs started flying, and Gene was again loudly doubting that God was going to help us survive. Alfred started yelling back, telling Gene he had ruined the power of the prayer with his swearing. I had to do something.

"Shut up!" I yelled at both of them.

I figured action was more important than words at this point, so I got them to move to more sustainable positions. Repositioning ourselves to get as much of our bodies out of the water as we could was only logical, so Alfred and I helped Gene up toward the bow of the boat. First, we got him alongside the keel, then he threw his leg over the top until he was sitting on it like he was riding a horse. Using anything I could for leverage, I pushed his backside so he reached the highest point. Gene lay down atop the boat's exposed and rocking hull and spread his arms out to hold on, trying to keep his balance and, at the very least, delay the onset of hypothermia.

The boat wasn't big to start with, but now all but a sliver of the skiff was underwater. I held the cooler in one arm and floated next to it, looking for something more stable to hold on to. The saving grace was the flats boat design, which had the stainless-steel frame of the poling platform in the back. I was fortunately able to stand on the frame and the platform and regained my footing in water that was up to my waist and climbed past my chest when I sat down. The position of the skiff's forty-horsepower engine provided stability. I looked around to make sure everyone was safe, make sure Gene was still holding on to the hull. I spotted Alfred in the water gripping the bow.

We'd just dumped two Styrofoam coolers worth of seafood into the water, effectively chumming for predators, but I wasn't thinking about sharks in that moment; I was thinking about the elements.

The rain was cold but the water was colder. I suddenly became aware of the water's temperature, and it worried me. When I moved, air bubbles that were trapped in my clothing shifted, allowing the water to hit my skin. Before this trip I would never have believed Bahamian water could feel colder than Long Island Sound in March. Submerged in the Abaco water, I started to shake. And at that moment I realized that it wasn't just the water that was cold—I thought I was beginning to slip into shock.

Gene and Alfred were on the bow, I was on the stern, and most of the boat between us was underwater. I was trying to think about what to do. My face was wet with salt water, some of it from the waves and the rest from tears formed out of the very real possibility that I wasn't going to survive this.

Trying to hold on to smooth, wet fiberglass is like trying to climb up a mirror. If there's nothing to grip, it's impossibly slippery. If there was one thing to be thankful for, it was that I had been pitched far away when the boat flipped. Had the hull landed on me, I would have been knocked unconscious and drowned. All of us were fortunate we hadn't broken bones, which would have made it impossible to hold on to the wet fiberglass.

Above the noise of the wind I could hear claps of thunder in the distance. They were upwind and loud, but I was confused by the sound being carried downwind to us. Then the lightning started, which I estimated at five or maybe six miles away, complicating our plight even further. In the water, hanging on to a metal platform made us a great lightning rod.

"Hey guys," I yelled. Even though they were only a few feet away, they couldn't hear me with the wind. "Guys!"

"What?!" I heard Gene respond.

I paused. Was I really going to tell them that if a lightning bolt hit the water it would be all over? Is that how we should all spend our final few minutes alive? Did they not notice it themselves and know in their hearts that we were about to die? I didn't need to reinforce that reality as I counted the seconds between flashes to determine how close the lightning was to us.

"You okay up there?" I asked instead.

"We're okay," Gene said. "What about you?"

"I'm okay," I said. "But we've got to balance the boat, or it's going to roll over and throw us off. Get in the middle!"

Gene slid down so Alfred could get onto the bow while I stayed in the back. It was the only way we could make things work. The bow was riding higher out of the water, the stern was submerged, and we weren't drifting.

"Remember that book *Unbroken*?" Gene asked suddenly.

He was a voracious reader. I was familiar with the book because I'd seen the movie about the incredible story of survival. He started telling Alfred and me the whole story of how World War II airman and Olympic athlete Louis Zamperini survived on a raft at sea after being shot down. Gene had meant for the story to be inspiring and reassuring, but all it did was remind us of the dire nature of our plight. I tuned him out, while letting Gene drone on because it was making him feel better.

I wondered why the boat didn't just sink completely. These skiffs weren't known for being buoyant, so we were fortunate it was still somehow clinging to the surface. What, though, was keeping it and us afloat?

I became obsessed with answering that question, and then it dawned on me: there was air trapped in the bow storage box where we'd found the grappling hook. A pocket of air was keeping us alive. For the first time in a long while I looked to the sky I smiled, a hefty portion of my faith restored. Now I just had to hope that pocket of air held . . . and we didn't spot any shark fins on the water's surface.

I saw Gene floundering and knew I had to do something fast. The only thing I could do to help him was to remove the extra pair of rain pants that I wore to prevent hypothermia. I tied one end of them to the bow hook and managed to get the other end to Gene.

"Tie this to your wrist!" I told him.

Gene was riding the bow of the boat like a bronco, swaying from side to side. But tying the other end of the pants to his wrist would now prevent him from rolling off into the sea. I could see Alfred bobbing in the water, holding fast to the bow. We were all safe for the moment.

But how long would the moment last?

17

KNOT NORMAL

It was pitch black out, the wind was blowing, and the chop kept crashing against the fiberglass boat—the furthest things imaginable from the comfort of home and family. I thought about my wife and my kids, and for the first time since I'd called home that morning I dwelled on what home meant to me. The kids were on school vacation. It was about eight o'clock, which meant dinner was over and they were all settling in to whatever they had planned for the evening. I pictured my wife sitting on the couch, reading a book or watching some television with the dogs curled up at her feet. The kids might be hanging out with her and chatting about school and friends and sports. They also might be in their rooms watching a movie or over at a friend's house talking about things like prom, commencement, or their plans for the summer.

I thought about how much I loved my home, particularly my family room that Gene helped me to build a few years before. I had always wanted a family room where I could surround myself with everything I like, so we created a vaulted ceiling with exposed beams and I hung enough duck mounts from the beams to make it look like an incoming skein of ducks. Instead of picking one species of bird,

I mixed and matched puddle ducks and diver ducks and sea ducks, all representative of the kinds that I hunted from my blind when I was a boy. Elsewhere in the room, I added books, fish mounts, and a caribou mount to go along with carvings and artwork. Every time I went into that room I felt peaceful and comfortable, in stark contrast to the miserable situation I was currently in.

Then I thought about my son Donald and wondered what was going through his mind back at the lodge. I imagined how nervous he must be, tried to put myself in his head and imagine what he was thinking and doing. It had been four or five hours since I'd spoken with the lodge manager on the phone, and enough time had passed that everyone would know something had gone terribly wrong. Putting my son in a position where he'd have to worry about his dad struck a nerve with me. That wasn't the proper role for a son Donald's age; a parent is supposed to protect his children and shield them from pain, not subject them to it. Worry and anxiety were what a parent was supposed to feel.

My son and I spent enough time on the water for him to know what it's like, having ventured hours far offshore to catch game fish. He knew what it was like to be running back to home port in the dark. But now it was well past sunset. The boats were not all accounted for, and neither was the crew. He had to know something was wrong, but what could he do about it? I pictured the despair he must be feeling over not being able to do anything helpful or constructive. That had to be weighing heavy on his heart, and when I felt that burden my breath caught in my throat.

A particular calmness fell over me around midnight, though. Suddenly, I wasn't worried about a thing. I didn't feel like I was in the water, and my body felt weightless. The wind was howling, and it was in that pitch blackness that I started to think about my friend Jimmy, who ran the local funeral home and was practically family. Under his direction, every funeral was perfectly orchestrated, and he had a wonderful way of working with people who have suffered terrible losses. He was surrounded by death and grief every day of every week and yet was a gentleman in every way, an all-around wonderful human being.

I figured that I'd next meet Jimmy when he unzipped my body bag.

I wouldn't be looking up at him; I'd be looking down at him or looking at him from the side, in some otherworldly capacity. I'd watch him unzip the bag and roll my corpse onto the table. I'd watch him prepare to embalm my body, dress me in proper attire, and place me in a casket. If all went well and I wasn't too banged up, my funeral would be open casket where folks could walk up, pay their final respects, and move on to make room for the next mourner. Then the lid would be closed and my coffin placed in a hearse and delivered to our family plot to be placed in the ground for all eternity. I was glad it would be Jimmy handling all the details. I had every confidence he would do as great a job for me as he did for all families.

That is, if my body was ever found. If we were swept out to sea and I was washed away, my body might never be recovered. That meant my family would never have any closure. They would never have the peace of mind knowing that I was truly dead and buried, and that would haunt them for the rest of their lives. Or I could fall victim to sharks or some other ocean predator or scavenger. In that scenario, there wouldn't be much for even a mortician with Jimmy's skills to work with.

All of that intense thinking made me move around a bit, and when I did my foot hit the transducer at the bottom of the boat. It was connected to the depth finder by a cable, which sent and received the sonar waves to measure water depth. I ducked under the waves, reached down, and latched on to the thin cable, more like a thick wire, and sought the best angle from which to tear it from its mount. Then I resurfaced and tied one end to my waist and the other end to the Yeti cooler I thought still contained our lunches and some bottles of water, as well as the platform itself, threading everything together.

I was now able to prop the cooler before me at chest level, close enough to use as a rest for my arms by laying my elbows atop it. Our situation was so precarious that I didn't even dare open that cooler for fear it might jostle the boat enough to rob us of the precarious balance we'd claimed, which meant the contents were useless no matter how hungry or thirsty I grew. Beyond that, I could die now secure in the knowledge I was making things as easy for my family as possible, because I was effectively lashed to the skiff. That way, if I died my body would float alongside the vessel, and when rescuers found our wreckage they'd find my body intact, so long as the predatory fish didn't find me first. Small consolation, I know, but also a small victory of sorts in an evening riddled with defeat.

When I was done, I settled in to wait. My eyes stung from the salt running into them. I had been rubbing the skin around my eyes and face, and the combination of raw skin and salt caused me to wince with every wave.

On top of that, it was pitch black. The low cloud ceiling stripped away any light from the moon or stars. There was something surreal about looking around and not being able to see anything at all, as if the world began and ended at the skiff to which we were clinging. Nothing else existed beyond the darkness that enveloped us.

One question that ran through my mind amid that despair was, *Does anyone ever heed the warnings that they get in life?* We put ourselves in harm's way daily to do the things we need to do, as well as the things we love to do. We drive to work in traffic despite the frequency of fatal traffic accidents, or we board commuter trains where the engineer might be intoxicated, or get on an airplane with no certainty it has been properly maintained. We take all that for granted. The only time we realize the inherent danger of such simple acts is when they claim someone else's life, and then we dismiss that with feelings of good fortune that it wasn't us before vanquishing it from our consciousness. It's an odd way of thinking and of feeling, but we can blame human nature for that, the same way we can for all the rubbernecking that goes on in the aftermath of a car accident, where passing drivers slow in the complacent reality it wasn't them. We take so much for granted, including life itself. And normally, when tragedy comes it's fast and unavoidable, as opposed to the slow and lingering process we were experiencing lost at sea amid the utterly black night.

We usually have our guard up during normal times back home. The times we should be more aware of our situation, though, we tend to become more relaxed. We trust our drivers and our captains and our airline pilots, even though we know nothing about their relative competence, history, or records. Would you be comfortable getting into a livery car driven by someone with a DWI on their record? Or maybe a better question might be, have you ever asked someone driving you for their detailed driving record, or if they have enough gas in the tank to get you where you're going, before climbing into the back seat of their car?

Meanwhile, we were drifting on the predation line, where sharks and who knew what else might be lurking below. I was cold, wet, and lashed to an overturned boat to make my body at the very least recognizable when what seemed like the inevitable came to pass. I wasn't the captain of this boat; I was just a fisherman on board. But had I contributed to our plight by getting caught up in the moment to find a pot of golden fish at the end of a figurative rainbow? Why hadn't I asked Alfred how far away Moore's Island actually was? Why hadn't I paid more attention to the distance we were traveling instead of busying myself with tying knots?

No, Alfred, I could have said, *we've gone too far. Turn back.*

None of this ever would have happened had I managed that simple task, rooted in the careful planner and organizer I believed myself to be. Apparently, though, I had left that part of myself back in the lodge, making a terrible short-term choice to avoid wallowing in another day's lack of fish on a trip that had produced no bounty. Was catching a few bonefish worth risking my life over? Since the answer was clearly no, how was it I had stepped so broadly out of character?

I wasn't going to be like the businessman who perishes talking on his cell phone on the drive to work or the train commuter reading the newspaper when his train crashes headlong into another on the same track. I had only myself to blame for being mired in the dark and the cold, with no hope, having lost my claim on tomorrow.

I was tired. All I felt like doing was drifting off to sleep. I closed my eyes and couldn't feel the chill of the water anymore, my mind going as empty and dark as the seas around me.

18

WISHING UPON A STAR

When my face hit the cooler water, I woke up. I looked around to make sure that Gene and Alfred were still on the boat. I could see Gene easily enough because he was only ten feet away, but I had to look a little harder to find Alfred, who was hanging off the bow, his grip appearing secure. He had his back to me, and his jacket was dark.

I breathed a sigh of relief, but otherwise, calming my nerves wasn't easy. My heart was racing and adrenaline coursed through my veins. I breathed deeply to chase away the deeper anxiety that had greeted being roused so suddenly. When that failed, though, I decided to embrace it.

Most people, of course, want to avoid anxiety at all costs. It raises blood pressure, leads clearheaded people to become thoughtless and reactionary, and contributes to making mistakes. I've suffered anxiety issues all my life, so I'm no stranger to knowing how to calm myself down. But none of those trusted techniques worked in the midst of drifting at sea while clinging to a capsized boat, so I ended up harnessing the anxiety to keep me alert and in full grasp of the dire plight I was in. As a result, I didn't miss anything—whether it be a threat or a potential service to our cause, which was bleak at best.

I thought about a time many years ago when I was riding the railroad. The train I was in broke down before we reached Manhattan, and there was an announcement over the PA that we needed to disembark and catch another one. I noticed a man in a wheelchair in the same car as me. We rode the same train a lot, and I've got to tell you, he wasn't the nicest guy. But I watched everyone brushing by him with their newspapers and briefcases, like he wasn't there at all. I knew I had to do something, but that meant enlisting others to help me get him into the station. I took him into my arms and signaled others nearby to handle other tasks, like taking charge of his wheelchair. Once on the platform, I now had to carry him up the long set of stairs so he could catch the next train. Someone else followed, carrying his jacket and briefcase. Another person toted his wheelchair. It was like an assembly line, and it might never have happened if I hadn't stepped up to help this guy everyone else was ignoring. But I couldn't do it alone, just like the three of us needed to work together to survive the night. What good would a rescue do when daylight came if we were all dead already? If we could keep hanging on, though, I felt certain there would be someone coming to look for us now that our return to Bay Lodge was long overdue.

"Where's the *fooking* cavalry?" Gene asked, as if reading my mind.

"I'm sure de'll call my cousin," Alfred said. "He knows a path I take to get to Moore's. Der probably on der way to find us right now."

While I wanted to believe his statement, I knew it wasn't true. We had drifted hopelessly off course through the stretch of time since we'd left Moore's Island. The whole day it had been like a desert on the sea, with not a single aircraft or boat to be seen. We were on our own, left to fend for ourselves. No one was coming, and that realization struck me hard and fast, leaving an empty feeling in the pit of my stomach. At night, in a storm this powerful, no plane would be able to spot us on the surface, and no rescue boat would be able to find us. And even if we knew our precise position, there was no way to communicate that to the lodge or the Coast Guard.

We had been in the water for several hours, and there was no sign of help in sight—no other boats, no fishermen, and no lights. I didn't hear the whine of an outboard or the spin of a plane's propeller. All I heard was the wind and the waves slapping against the boat's hull and then the sound of a brief shriek as Gene slipped off the capsized skiff.

At first, he was facing away from me, and then he flipped over. He started drifting past me; his eyes were wide and his white hair was wet and disheveled. I reached out to grab him, and when I did, it wasn't Gene's face I saw . . .

It was my father's, as if I could save the life cancer had taken when I was in my twenties.

I detached myself from the transducer line lashing me to the skiff and swam toward Gene. I grabbed hold and pulled him back toward the boat and helped him get back on by putting my head in his crotch from behind and lifting on an angle that wouldn't flip the boat. Gene was indeed a bull of a man, but after so many hours of trying to maintain his balance he got tired and slipped into the water. He didn't struggle or speak when I helped him, and I could tell he was on the verge of giving up. And I didn't blame him for that, because I wasn't far behind.

When I moved back down into my position, I reattached the transducer line, then propped myself back up on the stern and breathed a sigh of relief. Thoughts of my father flooded my mind like I was watching a series of scenes from different phases in my life, a side effect of prolonged exposure in the salt water and having swallowed a lot of it, resulting in my delusional thinking. Some of my thoughts were good, more were mixed, and still others were downright sad.

Suddenly, I was lying on my hospital bed again just after my duck hunting accident. Most of the voices I heard at that time were a blur, and my memories of the people and their faces were fuzzy at best. What was crystal clear in this vision, memory, or whatever was when my father walked into the emergency room and confronted the doctor in as direct a fashion as I can ever remember him speaking.

"I don't care what it costs," he told the doctor. "Save his leg."

"Mr. Denihan," the doctor said, "it's not about saving his leg. That's up to God now."

"Then you can find me in the chapel," my father said. "Now please save his leg."

At that point I remember closing my eyes. The sounds grew lower, the bright lights grew dim, and I drifted off to sleep.

Dad has it under control, I thought. *Everything is going to be just fine*.

Then I had a vision of my father laid out in his casket at his wake. So many people had come, and it was the first time I realized just how many people knew my father. There were lines out the funeral home door and people just kept coming, wave after wave, to pay their respects. Until he had died I never realized how many lives he touched and how many people he influenced across all walks of life. Mixed in with CEOs of Fortune 500 companies were street sweepers and sanitation workers—basically hardworking everyday people—who impressed my father just as much as the wealthy and powerful. Everyone spoke fondly of him, which made me proud that he had crossed social boundaries and was friends with people from all walks of life.

I admired my father and never wanted to disappoint him. I wanted him to be proud of me. He valued achievement above all else, so I constantly tried to do things to gain his approval, but I never felt that I had really lived up to his standards. I never felt that I came close to his expectations for me. Letting down the man I admired the most was a constant sore spot in my life, and now I felt I'd disappointed him again by being stuck at sea and facing the real possibility I would let my family down by not returning alive.

I started talking to my father as if he were there. I told him that I had spent my life trying to do good things and I felt that mine was a life worth living. I believed I'd been kind to people, that I was generous with my time and my feelings toward them. I told my father that before I made a serious decision I would ask myself, *What would Dad do?* I felt that he was with me always and that I knew he loved me even though he never expressed it the way the fathers of my friends did. I told him that I had grown into a man who was a lot like him, though inwardly I wondered if I'd be seeing him soon.

I took my dad out on my boat for rides around the bay on Sundays after church. He wasn't much of a fisherman. I knew he wouldn't have blamed me for this, even though I blamed myself.

I was named after my father's brother, and in my family that meant a lot. I never met my uncle because he died six months before I was born, but I was his namesake and therefore had big shoes to fill. My father expected a lot of all of us. Part of me believed that I was expected to keep his brother's memory alive.

Ironically, I was more like my father than my uncle, from what I'd been told. For all his stoicism and gruffness, I'd later learn my father had been very distressed in the aftermath of my hunting accident. From what my mom says he paced the floors until he practically wore the wax off the tiles. He pushed the doctors and nurses, even the priests, to focus their full attention in thought, word, prayer, and deed on my recovery. And then he worried whether the lingering effects of the accident would curtail me living a full life, that maybe if he had found better doctors, a better hospital, better treatment, the prognosis might have been different.

My father cut no more slack for himself than he did any other family member. After pressing sheets in the laundry as a young boy,

I started running errands and then working in the bowels of the hotels in my teens. In my early twenties, around the time my dad was bedridden in the downstairs of our house, I began overseeing important contract negotiations.

If he could only see me now, I thought, *sitting in the Abaco waters, strapped to an overturned boat with no rescue in sight. I can only imagine what he'd say . . .*

I'd always wanted a relationship with my father, but it never happened. It was particularly important to me after my hunting accident; if nothing else, I wanted to hear him say that he wasn't mad at me, that he was proud of how hard I worked to rebound from my gunshot wound. I wanted him to know that it was just an accident, and that I learned from it and moved on. I wanted him to know that I pushed hard every day to walk and to get back to a normal life. I wanted him to know that I appreciated all his efforts and that I knew how much he cared for me.

We were at a family gathering at our house one night after my hunting accident when I was fully charged by emotions, and I went up to him and told him what I thought of him.

"Dad," I said, just short of my seventeenth birthday.

"Yes, son."

"I love you."

There was a long pause. His eyes welled up.

"Go to bed," he said.

All these thoughts swam in my head as I fought to stay alert on the stern of the overturned boat. The darkness all around was like being in a closet, and all I wished for was to see a little light. It didn't matter where it came from or what kind of light it was, but I needed to see something other than blackness.

Then I thought I saw something odd in the water and realized it was a cormorant swimming nearby, a shiny black bird atop the pitch-black water. If I looked at it straight on, it was invisible, but if I looked at it from the side its shape became clear.

In that moment, I felt that my father was with me. I felt his presence, and a calmness settled over me. He was watching out for me, just as he had at the hospital, so amid the hopelessness I'd felt just moments before I started talking with him.

"Dad," I started, "I've done a lot of good things in my life. I feel that I have lived my life, and I have worked hard and taken care of everyone as best I could. I'm not sure how everything is going to turn out, but however it does it will be the way God wants it to."

I started to say more Hail Marys. Nothing happened after the fourth one, but as I finished my fifth the moon came out. The light in the sky brightened everything up, and I knew that my father was giving me a sign to keep my spirits up. I could see the bow of the boat and Alfred, I could see Gene holding fast again ten feet away, and I could see the sudden wash of luminescent light dancing on the water. I went back to my Hail Marys.

Once again, nothing happened after my fourth Hail Mary, but after my fifth the rain stopped. Not that we'd be able to dry out given how soaked we were. But at least it meant that the heavens were quieting down and that the moonlight and clear skies indicated the storm was passing. We were able to see more than we had in hours, and the storm had abated for the first time since the sun went down. The heavens were smiling on us at long last.

And then I saw a shooting star.

The star raced through the sky from left to right. It left a brief trail as it whizzed past some of the other stars that had popped out since the clouds cleared. I watched it with fascination as the bright light faded away and thought about the happy times associated with seeing a shooting star. As kids we'd all make wishes and believe that each and every one would come true. On clear nights we'd search high in the sky for a shooting star, all the while waiting to launch a wish.

I had only one wish to make that night.

19

RESCUE

After I made my wish, my jumbled thoughts turned to my mother. She was tough, a real-life version of Rosie the Riveter who worked assembling bombers used in World War II. Her inspection number was attached to every plane that left the assembly line for the tarmac, and she took her job very seriously. Whenever a plane went down with mechanical problems during the war, she meticulously researched the inspection numbers to see if it had been one of her planes. In all her years of work, none of her planes experienced a structural failure, and that was a source of great pride for her. I thought of that fact in this moment, because it defined her attitude about taking care of our family. While Dad taught us about business, Mom taught us to fix things.

I only wished she could fix this, now that my father had cleared the sky and let the moon shine through. It was the time to rally the troops, stay positive, and figure out what we needed to do to make it through the night. If we managed that much, the rising sun would bring us hope for a rescue.

Being in the water gave me a lot of time to think, as well as to feel. The experience enveloped me in solitude. I was thinking and feeling things that hadn't crossed my mind in decades. It allowed me to realize that many issues had been left unresolved. It was good for me to think about my father, my mother, my foot, my prostate cancer—basically, my entire life. I saw my own family from a different perspective, which illuminated all their wonderful qualities that I too seldom focused on, fixating instead on what they did wrong. While in the water, I realized how much I loved them all and how I would be lost without them. The possibility of impending death revealed all of this to me as I thought of the incredible love I shared with my wife, kids, siblings, nieces, nephews, and friends. The day-to-day shuffle has a way of muting those feelings by focusing on what is wrong, but in those moments beneath the spill of the moonlight, all I could feel was what was right.

I wanted to be back at the Bay Lodge. I wanted to have a drink, take a hot shower, put on some dry clothes, and catch a few hours of sleep. The next morning, I wanted to fly straight to New York and be home. As soon as I got there, I wanted to tell my wife and kids how much I loved them and how important they were to me. I saw this whole experience as a golfing mulligan, a second chance to get everything right.

A pipe dream for sure, especially when all I heard was the wind and the waves still slapping against the hull. Home suddenly seemed very far away again. Why hadn't we been rescued by now? There were clearly no searchlights coming from helicopters and no distant whine of engines from rescue boats cruising the horizon. We still didn't have any self-rescue gear, no warm clothes and no way of letting anyone know where we were. But I thought we should still have some food and water in the Yeti cooler that had been supporting my upper body through the long night. By the break of dawn, the seas had calmed enough for me to open it, and I lifted the top slowly and cautiously, still cognizant that the slightest jostle could lead to disaster.

The cooler was empty. The sandwiches and bottles of water I'd expected to be inside had been shed by the storm into the sea hours before. The moment devastated me. Thoughts of opening that cooler to reveal the bounty inside had sustained me through the night. The life saver we needed to survive another day didn't exist, and there was now no way we could stay hydrated.

Feeling helpless, believing that no one was coming for us, shook me to the core. As a safety nut, how had I allowed this to happen? I usually kept a to-go bag at the ready that included GPS, emergency beacons, first-aid kit, thermal blankets, satellite phone, and more. Not only did I have none of that with me now, I had ventured out in a skiff that lacked even the basic safety standards any boat should be equipped with. It was easy to blame Alfred, except for the fact there were questions I hadn't bothered to pose, especially once we set off on a thirty-mile jaunt for Moore's Island which, of course, necessitated covering an equal distance back in a skiff that didn't even have any of the safety gear that should have been on board.

What had I been thinking?

"Where's the *fooking* cavalry?" Gene wondered again, his Irish brogue stronger than ever.

"Gene," I said, "you've got to relax. Help will be on the way."

That's exactly what I said, and no sooner were the words out of my mouth than I wondered why I bothered staying strong for him when I wasn't able to do the same for myself. I didn't buy my own assurances, so why was I uttering them? Who was I trying to fool, Gene or myself? My thoughts swayed from the reassuring presence of my father to the fact that I didn't even have my rosary beads to bring me comfort.

Maybe that's where the blame lay.

Through my despair, I knew at some point the sun would rise, and with it would come hope. I longed for a new beginning, because our current plight signaled a near inevitable end, and I had faith I would live to see that light. Only my faith could replace the lonely, desperate, fearful, and helpless emotions that plagued me. We needed to hold out until the magical beauty of the sun returned to light the sky.

The thought made me smile for the first time since the sun had set hours before. After nearly submitting to our plight, I now trusted myself and needed to share my strength with Gene and Alfred so that they too would feel the hope that I felt. Unfortunately, other than our stop at Moore's Island, we hadn't seen another person, boat, or airplane cruising overhead all day. We were in no-man's-land and couldn't rely on any remote notion of the cavalry coming to our rescue. Clinging to the boat, meanwhile, was taking a tremendous toll on us. Picture extending your arm while holding a full cup of coffee, then see how long you can hold it with an outstretched hand before your shoulder and arm begin to tire. Now, imagine doing that for nearly a dozen hours.

In the darkest of moments, when rescue seemed not to be in the cards, I had failed to consider the ace we had in the hole.

Over the years I had taught my son Donald everything about fishing and boating, and in particular about safety on the water. Every time we went out on the boat, we went through a system so that we'd be prepared for any situation we might encounter. So even though Donald was only twenty-two, he boasted a wealth of experience that made him an accomplished boater and angler. (Today, he's a licensed captain.) He knew firsthand about the conditions because he had been out fishing that day in the fog, the rain, the thunder and lightning storms. By seven o'clock that night, when we were two hours overdue, he would have known something was very wrong. And he was virtually certain to contact my brother Laurence, who was in nearby Miami on vacation.

Launching a search and rescue mission seemed like it should have been an easy and obvious thing to do. When someone has direct knowledge that a boat is in distress, they call the authorities responsible for dispatching rescue teams. If your car breaks down on the highway, call a tow truck. If there is a fire in your home, call the fire department. In case of a medical emergency, call 911. It all seems so very simple, but when you're dealing with territories that have different governing bodies, it can get complicated and political very quickly.

To resolve situations like that, you need someone who is tenacious, has a clear idea of how to align the different groups, and possesses the ability to cut through all the red tape to get it done. That described my brother Laurence to a T. Nothing was going to stop him and Donald from getting all possible rescue efforts launched on our behalf. In our darkest moments, I clung to that belief as tightly as I held fast to the boat.

Laurence, I'd later learn, cleared the first hurdle by creating a joint partnership. The U.S. Coast Guard has jurisdiction in American waters only, while the Bahamas Air Sea Rescue Association, BASRA, services the Bahamas. A second hurdle was that the Coast Guard was a branch of the United States military and is federally funded, while BASRA was a nonprofit organization. A third issue was the available resources. The Coast Guard enjoyed a long-standing, rich history at sea and maintained a large, well-trained corps with boats, planes, and helicopters, while BASRA had limited staffing and resources. The BASRA folks were all volunteers who worked only on a part-time basis. So, a bridge needed to be built between the two bodies to initiate the rescue effort, and thanks to my brother that's exactly what was happening.

Phone calls and emails flew until Laurence was successful connecting the Coast Guard with BASRA, establishing a cooperative relationship. Within three hours of receiving Laurence's call, a Coast Guard helicopter lifted off from Miami headed for Abaco. They undertook a grid search based on the coordinates my son had provided. The search and rescue helicopter covered most of Abaco and the smaller cays until around 2:45 a.m., when they needed to call off their mission due to low fuel and duty times, because the same crew had handled a drug interdiction at sea earlier in the evening. It turned out I had actually heard the Coast Guard helicopter circling but took the distant *wop-wop-wop* for thunder.

BASRA did not have the aircraft to conduct a night search, so they planned for a morning deployment, at which point they dispatched a fifty-three-year-old volunteer pilot named Vic Williams. Vic would be flying with a twenty-five-year-old spotter named Aaron Banks in Williams' private plane.

In the meantime, Laurence left no stone unturned. While waiting for daylight to come he hired seaplane and bush pilot Rick Riley to be deployed for the actual rescue. The Coast Guard made the initial search and communicated their results to BASRA, who would then take over during daylight hours. If BASRA was lucky enough to find us, they would communicate our GPS coordinates to Rick, who would be wheels up at 7:30 a.m. when the light was sufficient. Laurence had all those elements covered, while my son Donald would lead the search by boat if the planes were unable to find us.

Everything on the water is linked together. The tides, the lunar phases, the seasonality, the water temperatures, the wind direction, the structure and depths, and the baitfish all move in a purposeful way. Predator fish move in at the appropriate times to feed, to migrate, to breed, and to rest. Birds are an important part of that mix, and if you study them you'll know what's taking place on the water. Terns like small baitfish, gannets favor herring, shearwaters like squid, and so on.

That made me think about the cormorant from a while ago. Those dark, greasy birds do not stray too far from shore. I realized that was a sign I should have paid attention to earlier. The bird was hard to see amid the pitch-black night because its black feathers blended in with the low light and the choppy water, but I had known what it was all the same.

Thinking about that cormorant now gave me hope that we were closer to land than I had originally gauged. I didn't detect any land when our flats boat was still afloat, because the visibility was so poor, hampered by a blanket of thick clouds and black skies, further roiled by the driving rains. When the boat flipped, it was all I could do to put us in position to survive, paying no heed to our surroundings since we weren't going anywhere anyway. The cormorant, though, had proved itself to be a crucial harbinger, alerting me to the fact that we were close enough to land to significantly raise the odds of a rescue once the light came up. Although in retrospect, it may well have all been an illusion conjured by my subconscious to provide a measure of hope.

My spirits had lifted in the darkest hours of the night while the three of us clung desperately to whatever holds we could find to stay alive. Exhaustion had set in, and I began to fade in and out of consciousness. The next sight I saw upon rousing myself alert with the promise of dawn in the sky wasn't a cormorant at all.

It was my father's face.

His hair was white and his eyes were very wide. I could see his cheekbones and his prominent jawline, and I thought hard about when he had looked so gaunt and pale and drawn. Then I remembered: it had been when he was lying on a bed in our home, during the final few weeks of his life.

That was when my father was losing his battle to prostate cancer. We had his hospital bed placed in the very family room I had used after my hunting accident because I couldn't climb the stairs. Whereas, I had moved in there to recover, though, my dad had taken up residence to die. I spent a lot of time with him, and a part of me was really trying to find a way to comfort him now that treatment hadn't worked and hope had been lost. Anyone who's been in that position knows the helpless feeling that occupies every thought and emotion. Reconciling myself to the fact there was nothing I could do to help my father was difficult, and yet now he had appeared to help me.

My father was always there when I needed him the most. He made me the man I am today. He helped me build my career. Then, in his time of greatest need, there wasn't anything I could do to help him. At that time, even the best doctors in the world couldn't find a way to slow the progress of the disease that was ravaging him.

I wondered what all that meant. Was my father's image on the water a sign I was drawing near to him and would die soon? Or had he appeared to tell me to hold on just a little longer, that help was coming? My faith told me to believe the latter, and I became one with the darkness enveloping me with the promise of a day's new light ahead.

When you're in the ocean for a swim, you'll frequently get a mouthful of salt water. In small doses it can actually taste pretty good, sort of the way potato chips or peanuts go well with a beverage. If you're in the sea for quite a while, there is a pretty good chance you'll wind up drinking a decent amount, and that's when the hallucinations can kick in. Still, I clung to the hope that the vision of my father hadn't been a hallucination at all but a sign. I just didn't know for what yet.

My lack of sleep, the absence of food and fresh water, and the constant stress that had accompanied the struggle for survival left me utterly exhausted, so much so that I feared I'd never see the dawn. That I'd pass out and slip peacefully into the sea to greet eternity. It became a daunting task to hang on to the boat and tread water. But I'd come too far to quit now, and I found resolve in the belief that the appearance of my father was a sign that rescue efforts were afoot.

If I could keep holding on, clinging to life with the final reserves of my ebbing strength . . .

I don't know how much seawater I drank—heck, it could have been quite a lot. Whereas I was normally focused and resolved, I was now questioning and doubtful. I wondered if my arms were trembling because they had been holding on to the boat for Lord knows how many hours or if my body was beginning to shut down as a result of dehydration. I questioned if my vision was blurry from lack of sleep or from the salt. If I had a gallon of fresh spring water I would consume it in one gulp. Now when I looked around, I saw blue and white hues that reminded me of an umbilical cord.

Suddenly, the color of the water brightened ever so slightly, a transient light that meant dawn was an hour or so away. Having lost all track of time, the hours overnight had passed like days and the minutes like hours. Knowing the sunrise was coming and being able to wind a celestial clock by that certainty filled me with a resolve I hadn't felt since we'd capsized.

A predawn chill had settled on the water. It would not be a brilliant, colorful dawn like those I'd see back home when I headed out of the harbor and motored east toward Block Island. There would be no purple and magenta and yellow and orange and green colors surrounding the giant orange ball, thanks to the stormy weather that refused to relinquish its grip.

The sun, when it finally rose, was not visible through the gray clouds or the slate-colored sky. But I greeted even that meager light, little more than a sliver really, as a new beginning that brought fresh hope to us. As beaten down as I was, I knew we had faced the worst nature had to throw at us and had survived. And we had not survived the blackness of the night to die in the light of the day.

As the gray, dreary morning dragged, though, I started to wonder how much longer we could cling to the vessel. I knew that if the boat sank or we lost our grip on it we'd be adrift and at the mercy of the choppy seas, ingesting even more seawater and experiencing increased hallucinations and dehydration.

"Hey!" Gene shouted dryly out of nowhere. "Over there, look up, look up high! I can see a plane!"

I craned my head to try and locate it but could see nothing but gray skies through the drizzle seeping from the clouds. For a moment I thought Gene might be hallucinating, but then I spotted the distant speck of a small plane on the horizon, high in the air and still quite a distance away.

Gene shouted again, "Do you see it?"

"Yes!" I croaked, "but it's too high to see us!"

Still I felt some hope, knowing this plane might be searching for us.

"It saw us!" shouted Gene. "It tilted its wings! There it is! It tilted its wings again!"

I wasn't so sure. We watched the plane fly away from us. Maybe Gene was right, but the plane was leaving and I could hardly bear the thought that it hadn't spotted us.

What if that was it? I thought. *What if we'd just watched our one chance at survival soar away?*

But then I remembered Gene was studying to be a pilot, trained to do such things and, thus, to recognize them in a way I couldn't. I found hope in that realization but lost it when the plane didn't reappear in the sky. No more words were exchanged between us, because it took too much effort to shout above the wind. Instead we each retreated into our own thoughts and focused dejectedly on the task of continuing to hang on to the overturned skiff.

About fifteen minutes later, a bright hue emerged from the sky, a beaming, beautiful white light on the horizon that gave me peace from that first glance. It reminded me of Dorothy landing in Oz to find a world of magical color awaiting her. I thought I was either hallucinating or this was my final image before death and that we'd lost our battle against the sea. The light was drawing closer, and I followed it in transfixed fashion, still having not come to grips with what it might be or represent, or even if it was real given the delusions I seemed to be suffering from. I began to think that this beautiful glow on the horizon was light cast from heaven to welcome me there. I wondered if I should follow it, if my hold on life was ebbing.

Then a seaplane roared fifty feet over us and I made eye contact with the pilot, and that's when I broke down for the first time since this had all begun, tears streaming down my cheeks.

We'd been found!

I wondered what his next move would be. Given that the seas were so rough, I wasn't sure whether he could land the plane or just alert rescue boats to our position. This aircraft was much bigger than the one we saw in the distance earlier. But the pilot's expertise and familiarity with the waters allowed him to use the downward air pressure to touch down roughly on the choppy seas. He bounced and then positioned the aircraft precisely so that the water could do the work in drifting the plane toward us.

I thought for a moment he was moving so fast that one of the pontoons might crash into our capsized skiff and send us reeling anew. But he turned at the last moment and braked to an almost immediate halt alongside us. I was in a state of shock, euphoria, or some combination of the two. After all this, was our ordeal truly over?

Gene, Alfred, and I reached up to the most welcome hands we'd ever felt and climbed onto a pontoon and then onto a couple steps that led up into the plane. The pilot, Rick Riley, continued to work the controls while his wife Aviva and another rescuer helped us on board.

"There is a God!" I shouted.

Aviva laughed and handed me a bottle of water. It was the sweetest, purest taste I'd ever experienced. Then tears poured down my face.

We were saved.

As we flew back to the mainland, I learned my brother had hired the plane. Rick and Aviva explained that the small aircraft we had seen earlier was a volunteer aircraft for BASRA, and its pilot, Vic Williams, had indeed seen us and radioed our location, thanks almost solely to the efforts of my son and my brother.

I kissed the tarmac when we landed at Marsh Harbour Airport.

Gene slapped the remnants of his soggy bankroll, which had somehow survived our long ordeal at sea, into the pilot's hand.

"Take it," he said.

I remember how he'd planted another wad, plucked from the same pocket, in the hands of the fisherman back on Moore's Island for the spiny lobster and stone crab we'd purchased that were now long lost to the sea. I couldn't help but wonder whether Gene had some magical ability to conjure cash out of thin air. In that moment, it seemed the only explanation for how he had somehow held on to a wad thick enough to serve as a floatation device in its own respect.

Gene's legs were all torn up, almost like road burn, from clinging to the hull of that boat for dear life, but that wasn't the only thing that was scarred. Afterward, he told me, he'd been doing calculations through the night to determine when the air in the deck hold would leak out and leave us with nothing to hold on to. That's one reason why he had so little to say throughout those long, dark hours. Fortunately, though, his calculations had proven wrong.

"They were right," he told me. "I'm certain of it. We should be dead. There's no fooking explanation for it."

I thought of my dad and all the praying I had done, all the Hail Marys I'd recited.

There was an explanation, all right.

20

GOD IS GOOD

The feeling of stepping back on dry land (well, seashells mixed with concrete) of the runway was indescribable. After all we'd been through, it was all I could do not to break down. That would wait until my reunion with Donald, whose cool head had saved our lives.

My friend Harry, a giant of a man with a heart as big as his body, was waiting outside the tiny terminal smiling from ear to ear. He hugged me so tight it reminded me of the stone crabs lost during the ordeal, because it felt like I was being crushed by a claw.

"Hey," he said when we separated, "what happened to those lobsters we heard about? Don't tell me you lost them!"

And then he nearly crushed me a second time. The only thing I enjoy more than the company of my family is the company of friends like Harry, the kind of friends who join me on trips like this. We don't see each other all that often, but when we do we pick things up without missing a beat. They teach me things without realizing they're teaching me anything at all. We share an appreciation of life that stretches far beyond how much money we've got in the bank or our investment portfolios. I had met Harry in an airport and just hit it off with him, for no other reason than he was a really good person. And I befriended him and the others who'd joined me on this trip based on who they are, not what they have. Because it's not about the size of their wallets so much as the size of their hearts that matters. In those times, we're all friends and fishermen, defined by our common bond and purpose. Too often people engage with others because they feel they need to, as opposed to wanting to, which is the way it is for me. If you want to know who your true friends are, ask yourself who makes you feel like a kid again when you're around them.

Because I had made that call to Bay Lodge, my son had been smart enough to reach out to a friend of his who owned a local AT&T store to explain our plight. His friend kept calling the tech department until he got someone on the line in the middle of the night who finally listened.

"A customer is lost at sea," he explained. "I've got the time he placed his last call. I need you to ping the location to help find him."

That guy in AT&T's tech department was able to use that last call I'd placed to track my latitude and longitude, giving the Coast Guard at least a general sense of where we were. Absent Donald's ingenuity, we might never have been rescued because there would have been no way to narrow the search grid, so by the time they found us, it might have been too late.

Donald had headed out to sea at first light as part of the seagoing rescue effort and hadn't returned yet. I later learned he was still searching for us when he got word we'd been found and were en route back to the lodge. Before heading back in, the captain on the center-console twenty-five-foot boat he'd gone out on continued on to the skiff's location to tow it back. Not surprisingly, Donald was the one who jumped into the water and righted the skiff to enable that effort. He claims it was because he was the only one on board wearing a bathing suit, but I know he would have been the one who jumped into the water no matter what he was wearing.

I was kind of glad for the delay in our reunion because the sense of being safe, alive, and back at the lodge was overwhelming in its own right. Much better to enjoy my reunion with my son separate of that.

After I called my family to tell them I was okay, I broke down in the privacy of my room. I started shaking uncontrollably, almost like I was having a flashback or fearing the rescue had been a hallucination and I had actually died amidst our twenty-hour ordeal at sea. I grew short of breath, almost like I was suffering a panic attack.

I sat down on the side of my bed and steadied my breathing. Then I pinched and prodded myself to make sure I was still there and this wasn't the product of a delusion. Slowly, gradually, my breathing steadied and my heartbeat slowed. I lay back on the bed to ponder my good fortune and what I might take from the closest brush with death I had ever experienced. Before I could ponder much at all, though, I fell into a deep sleep where the world was warm, dry, and comfortable.

I thought I'd dream of my father, picking up where the delusions at sea had left off. Instead, though, I dreamed of my four children. As parents, we all want to do right by our kids. We want to protect them, keep them safe and secure. In a strange way, though, over the course of the past nineteen hours or so, our roles had been reversed. The son had saved the father, and as I excitedly awaited his return, I realized then and there that, at twenty-two and a college senior, Donald was ready to leave his mark on the world.

Interestingly enough, I learned the Coast Guard had barely participated in the search. A search and rescue helicopter had covered most of Abaco and the smaller surrounding cays until 2:45 in the morning. They had actually called my wife right around the time their helicopter did its brief search.

"Mrs. Denihan," the officer on the other end of the line said, "we're out looking for your husband and we will not stop until we find him."

Well, they had stopped, and they weren't the ones who found me. Thankfully, Rick Riley and his seaplane were more than up to the task, but only because of the relentless efforts of my brother Laurence. While I had been holding on to our capsized boat for dear life, he had been on the phone and computer throughout the night, talking and emailing nonstop to arrange a search and rescue operation as soon as Donald had informed him we were missing and then reported our approximate coordinates. When printed out, the emails stretched to around an inch thick.

FROM: Laurence
SENT: Wednesday, March 14, 2012, 9:30 PM
TO: Steve
SUBJECT: Helicopter

Steve
We have an issue with my brother in the Bahamas fishing. He's not returned from fishing yet and is 2 hours late. Do you have any resources in Miami etc that we could hire to go out and search the area around Abaco Island in the Bahamas? Not US water or space. Chopper with search light is key. I'm thinking a chopper out of Nassau.

Laurence followed up that email with this one to the same party just before midnight, answering a request for more information:

They went out of Bay lodge which would be marsh harbor. I think they were heading east in the cays off the coast. We did get a BASRA plane in the air and currently searching as well as a US Coast Guard chopper. Being his brother I would love to get as many resources up as possible. Can you get a search chopper up?

After which, "Steve" sent this email to a trusted contact in the Nassau government:

URGENT: NEED HELICOPTER FOR SEARACH NEAR ABACO

NEED ANY HELICOPTER OPERATOR IN BAHAMAS FOR SEARCH MIS-
SION. Client has a brother on a fishing trip who is missing. Looking
to augment search with chartered helicopter.

Then Laurence sent this email the following morning:

On March 15, 2021, at 7:24 AM, Laurence wrote:

The search plane is taking off in the next 10 minutes by the Bahamian Search and Rescue. The only thing encouraging is that this has
happened before and they did find the fishermen cold and miserable in their boat about 10 years ago. Bahamian Search and Rescue
said that the guide might have stopped and set anchor once it got
dark since you can't see and it's more dangerous to try an advance
at night, or they could have plain run out of gas. US Coast Guard
said these things usually resolve themselves quickly once first light
happens. I have a private chopper in Nassau I'm working to get in
the air as well.

When this was all over, I sent BASRA a generous donation specifically to thank volunteer pilot Vic Williams, who'd spotted us and
directed Rick Riley to our position.

I can only imagine, meanwhile, how good it felt for Laurence to
pen this final email at 9:45 the morning of the rescue to those who
had been there for him every step of the way throughout the search:

They found them and your contact in Nassau was exceptional and
they are now aboard their seaplane and almost back to the lodge.
They should be at the lodge in 10 minutes. Thank you for the resources and your support. I will be back to you shortly on their need and
desire to get out of Abaco.

I didn't take my brother up on his offer to provide a plane to take me back home right away. I didn't want to leave at that point; I just wanted to chill for a day or two at the lodge to decompress and process everything I had been through.

This wasn't my first brush with death, after all, and I genuinely believe that the hunting accident when I was sixteen made me the man I am today. I had realized we're all on borrowed time at a very young age. Most people don't have that close a brush with death once in their lives, never mind three times as in my case. Being lost at sea and facing my own demise again helped further refine who I am, and it was important for me to pay proper thanks to all the people who had tried to help me, including the US Coast Guard.

A few months after that desperate night at sea, I flew back to Miami and met with the admiral who oversaw operations in the area stretching to the Bahamas, just to thank him.

He smiled reflectively. "You know, we've been fortunate enough to rescue a lot of people over the years, but you're the first one who ever came to our headquarters to thank us, and we weren't even the ones who rescued you."

The admiral's team took me through the step-by-step process of dividing the search area into grids and how the Coast Guard maximizes its resources with time so much of a factor. It made me feel that had it not been for them being stretched so thin that night, they might well have found me before Rick Riley did. Anyway, I wanted them to know I appreciated whatever effort they had made. As for Riley himself, I believed the sodden wad of cash Gene had gratefully pressed in his hand served as our demonstration of gratitude to him, especially since he'd done what he'd already been paid to do. But I stayed in touch with him, and whenever I see a seaplane cruising over my summer house, I think of Rick and his wife Aviva.

Incredibly, a few weeks after our ordeal, Gene opened a package back home to find the wallet he had lost at sea inside. It must have washed up on shore, where someone had found it and mailed it back to the address on Gene's driver's license.

"Look at this!" he said, shocked that someone would have taken the time and effort to send back a waterlogged wallet. "I don't fooking believe it!"

Gene's first thought was how he might thank the sender, but there was no return address. He hadn't exactly found God during our ordeal, but when he got home he did go to church regularly for a few weeks for the first time in twenty years. Then he lost interest and reverted back to his old habits, having moved on to other things. That's Gene.

I remembered my promise to Reverend Simms on Moore's Island, who was so taken with my Simms jacket because it bore his name. I told him I'd send him a matching jacket as soon as I got home, and that's what I did. I also promised Alfred that, if we survived, I was going to get him a new iPhone, which I also did. I felt so fortunate to be alive, I wasn't about to renege on any of my promises. The whole experience made me appreciate my life all the more and the people I've been fortunate enough to meet along the way, especially my wife and kids. It drew me closer to all of them, not just Donald, because I embraced the world I was fortunate to have around me.

The aftermath left me in contact with the lodge manager, not so much to rehash the events of that long night but to institute a system of measures to ensure at least the circumstances could never be revisited again. And I take great pride in the fact that our discussions led to the significant changes being implemented just two weeks later.

Beyond everything else, though, the experience also left me wanting to help others who truly needed that help, so I started the God Is Good fund, a 501(c)(3) dedicated to helping people in dire straits. After Superstorm Sandy, I contacted a local parish on Long Beach in Long Island, one of the hardest hit areas, and told them I wanted to help an elderly woman of their choosing to rebuild her home. The local priest told me about a woman, named Sandy incredibly, who fit the bill perfectly. Coincidence, someone once said, is another word for God.

Sandy had spent the night of the storm in her attic, but her son Bobby was confined to a wheelchair, and there was no way she could get him up that ladder. So Bobby ended up in water up to his chest when their one-story bungalow was flooded. Sandy herself was hearing-impaired and diabetic, so staying on the first floor with her son might have had dire consequences, and he had insisted he'd be okay and that she should ride things out in the attic—that way, she'd be better positioned to help him once the storm abated. Insurance would pay a measure of the cost for rebuilding their home, but far from all of it, and it would be months, even years, before they got started. So I stepped in.

I also stepped in when a couple in their thirties, Kerry and Chris (an event planner and firefighter respectively), with three young children, lost everything to the same storm. They spent a week crowded in a relative's home before finding a hotel room for a week near their ruined home in Long Beach. What, though, was going to happen to them from there, given that their modest ranch house was a total loss and no other housing alternatives they could afford were available?

They caught a big break when the owner of a vacant, fully furnished summer home stepped forward to offer lodging to a family in need. Miraculously, the place was close enough to the family's home so their children would be able to continue attending their current schools. Still, that solution was only temporary, and I stepped in with funding from God Is Good to rebuild their storm-ravaged home at no cost to them.

One of the most powerful experiences of my life was being taken on a tour of the decimated town that was little more than a barrier island that working-class people, many of them police and firefighters, had called home. Like me, many of them were of Irish descent. Now it was a disaster zone. Nearly every home had been flooded, their interiors riddled with mud and the stench of standing water that had soaked into the upholstery and carpets. Refuse in the form of kitchen stoves, drywall, children's toys, and mattresses spilled out of overflowing dumpsters that dotted the streets as constant reminders of the devastation visited upon this proud community.

I wish the God Is Good fund could have rebuilt every single one of those homes, but there was a limit to what I could do, and helping these two families would have to suffice and, hopefully, serve as a model for others to follow. As it was, the priest had arranged for me to tour both of these homes so I could choose one to rebuild.

"I can't choose, Father," I told him on the way back to the church. "I'll just have to take care of both."

But Kerry and Chris also had a disabled son, Connor, who was confined to a wheelchair and nearing his final battle with the neuromuscular disease that was killing him. Connor's final wish was to visit Disney World and meet Kermit the Frog. They had already scheduled the trip through the Make-A-Wish Foundation, but Superstorm Sandy had threatened to waylay their plans because of the logistical quagmire it had created, and Make-A-Wish had been unable to arrange for Connor to meet Kermit.

Fortunately, our very good friend Joanne had a media contact with close ties to Disney who was not only able to help get everything back on track but also facilitated Connor's dream of meeting with Kermit as well as having dinner in the Cinderella Castle.

"The trip to Disney World was the best of their lives," the *Associated Press* reported on December 12, 2021. "Connor had never been happier, bright and alert and grinning from ear to ear as he met the Magic Kingdom characters, Mickey and Woody and the Minions and, of course, Kermit. He went on carousel rides specially rigged for wheelchairs, splashed in the pool in his water chair and ate ice cream all day long."

Their rebuilt home wasn't finished when they got home, but they were back in it by the holidays. "This stranger walks into our lives and offers not just to rebuild our home, but to build us a better home," Kerry told the *Associated Press* for that same December 12 article. "It's absolutely a miracle."

I don't see it as a miracle at all. I see it as one person helping out others, because I couldn't live with the thought of Connor living out his final days in a motel room. Chris was a fireman who spent his life saving other people and now found himself on the other side, and it was a pleasure to come to his rescue, just as he had come to the rescue of countless others.

In both cases, the God Is Good fund rebuilt those families' homes. The fund paid for the materials, but my friends, associates, and kids all volunteered their time to perform these minor miracles for people who'd been kicked while they were down.

I hold myself to a very high standard, and my greatest weakness is the disappointment I feel when I see others settling for less from themselves. Almost dying that night at sea, not to mention years earlier in the hunting accident and then having to deal with the same dreaded disease that had killed my father, has taught me to put things in the proper perspective, and nothing disturbs me more than when somebody I know loses track of what's truly important in life. Too many people want to put a dollar sign on everything, perceiving everything as transactional instead of placing the greatest value in the relationships and interactions that define us as people. You can't really put a dollar sign on love, or happiness, or family, or friendship, or loyalty, but they're worth more than anything that comes with a price tag attached.

Well before that night at sea off Abaco, I had already encapsulated thoughts and beliefs like that into a mission statement that had only further crystallized in the aftermath of the boating accident:

> —*I'm a good husband, father, friend, and managing director. I am most at peace when I'm able to keep the above in balance.*

—I strive for purpose in my life, maintaining my sense of humor and enjoying stimulating interactions with others.

—I enjoy helping others achieve their goals.

—I'm challenged to be the best I can.

—I have a drive to accomplish much in a short period of time. I enjoy the process of building structures and teams.

—I often achieve goals through my path of continuous learning by continually asking the difficult/tough questions.

—I cherish the love and support of my family and seek to encourage their growth and development. I recognize that their goals may not be my goals. I appreciate their unique contributions to our family.

—Physical and mental health is highly valued by me. I strive to lead a life in balance, respecting the gifts God has given me.

I wrote that in 2000, twelve years before the boating accident. It defined my core then, and it reflects my core even more today. My father was thrown a bit when I told him I loved him at the age of sixteen. Today, I remind myself to make sure I tell people that I love them. Everybody's always bitching about something or other, but how often do you hear someone say "good job" or "thanks so much." I fully believe that if you do the right things, 99 percent of the time it will come back in a positive light to you. That's the way

I lived my life before, and the boating accident only strengthened that principle and reinforced my resolve to do more.

The epitaph on my tombstone should read, IS IT DONE YET? because that's my motto and encapsulates how I live every part of my life.

I had been back in my room in the lodge for a couple of hours, sometimes lying down and sometimes sitting in a chair while all the time replaying the events of the previous night. When a knock fell softly on my door, as if not wanting to disturb me if I'd managed to drift off to sleep, I knew it was my son Donald. Today, we're in business together, and he's running a project that will see us construct hundreds of homes down south. And we will take the same pride in building them that I did in rebuilding those two homes in Long Beach in the wake of Superstorm Sandy.

I opened the door to my room, and Donald practically leaped into my arms, both of us breaking down in tears. I don't think we ever hugged tighter or longer, both of us reluctant to let go as if the other might slip away like I almost had the night before.

Finally, I eased him away and looked into the still moist eyes of a young man about to graduate college and enter the next phase of life with the same vigor, enthusiasm, and resolve that had defined his twenty-two years up to that point. He was about to embark on the kind of journey I had around the same age when my own father had died. I couldn't have been prouder of him, just as I was sure my father had been proud of me. And I knew if I hugged him again, this time I might never let go, so I just held him by the shoulders at arm's distance.

"I love you, son," I said.

EPILOGUE

The Fishbowl

My response to the classic quandary of whether I'd do anything different if I had the opportunity to live my life over again may surprise you, because I wouldn't change a thing.

That may sound strange coming from someone who nearly lost his foot as a boy in a hunting accident and his life as a man at sea. Those incidents, along with surviving advanced prostate cancer, were hard bargains life made with me to help fashion the man I am today: the father, grandfather, husband, friend, man of faith, and businessman. I couldn't be happier having married the woman I married or raising the children we're blessed enough to have. Having faced so much adversity at a young age gifted me a perspective on life where I came to appreciate much of what everyone else took for granted. When walking up a simple set of stairs is like climbing Mount Everest, you learn to understand how fragile and short our years here can be.

Not all bargains in life are hard, but we don't learn nearly as much from the easy ones. Earlier in this book, I used a quote my father repeated often, "No morning sun shines all day." He said that to make the point that you should save your money—for a rainy day, to extend the metaphor. Now I realize my father could just as easily have been talking about life in general. Life is full of clouds, and storms, and darkness that serve to make us appreciate the light all the more. You don't come out ahead in every bargain you make, but you must strive to honor the terms, whether it be a bargain with an associate, a rival, a loved one, a friend, God, or even yourself.

See, in order to be a good winner, you've got to be a good loser. We like when life is quantifiable, when we can define success or failure by concrete numbers. In fishing it's about the number of fish you can catch, in golf it's about your handicap, and in school it's your grade point average (or GPA). But we can just as easily become prisoners of those numbers. Happiness is not something you can quantify with percentages and ratios. Too often we get lost in our own minutia, run over by a bus we're driving. That's what happens when you lose perspective, and if you take nothing else from this book, I hope it's how to gain that perspective back.

Much of this book was about fishing, at least as a backdrop for the second half. It makes me think of staring at fish through the glass of an aquarium. All day long people watch them swimming in and out of the rocks at the bottom of the tank through the oxygenated water to the top in search of the next meal. Consider the world from their point of view, though. To the fish, gazing out at us, you and I are living in a fishbowl too, and they probably feel worse for us than we do for them. And the more successful we become, the more money, status, and stuff we acquire, the more everyone wants to peer through the glass at us. Sometimes they want to see us drown and sometimes they're rooting for us to reach the top. But what matters the most isn't living life to please those people looking in, it's living life to please yourself while you're looking out.

When I looked out at the devastation left in the trail of Superstorm Sandy, I knew I had to do something. And I ended up helping Chris Troy, a firefighter whose career was about helping others but whom the storm rendered impotent in its wake when he needed to help himself. I was there for him, and his family, in their time of need, because he had been there so often for others in their time of need. Life is a circle, not a flat surface. It's easy to want to do great things when everybody's watching. The true measure of a person, alternatively, is how they behave and respond when nobody's watching.

Somebody always *is* watching, though, aren't they? We can see our reflections in our own personal fishbowls, and it's up to us to determine what those images bear. I started the God Is Good Fund in the wake of my near tragedy at sea, because the experience sharpened my view and broadened my outlook. It's not just about making a financial contribution, it's also about making an emotional contribution, of being present in the moment. Many people don't leave a tip until the server or attendant or whatever can see them do it. They do what they do for the recognition, while others simply tip because it's the right thing to do. They don't care if anyone's watching or not. They don't live their lives based on what they want people to see when they gaze into the fishbowl. And, to that end, I don't seek recognition; when the *Huffington Post* contacted me about the story they were doing on the Troys, I really didn't want to talk to them. Then I realized the story was about this wonderful family, not me, and that doing the interview might draw attention to the God Is Good Fund, so I'd be able to do more for people like the Troy's.

Everything in life is a bargain, and the most vital, defining ones are those we make with ourselves from inside the fishbowl instead of with those viewing us from the outside. I regard every act of kindness we are able to perform as a miracle. Like bargains, some are big and some are small, but all bear as much meaning to the one who makes the miracle as those who receive it.

Inside that fishbowl, we need to ask ourselves if we're happy or not. Happy with what we have and okay with what we don't. It shouldn't take a catastrophe to see ourselves differently, to realize that no matter how bad things get, someone else has it worse. And we shouldn't wait for a catastrophe to become a better person. When our reflection shines inside the fishbowl, it's okay to ask ourselves,

How can I be a better person? Because if I'm better person, it follows that I'll be happier.

After I got home from the Bahamas following my ordeal at sea, another of the people I reached out to thank was the dispatcher who'd sent the pilot Rick Riley up to search for us at sea.

"You just brought chills to my spine," she said, beyond grateful that I had acknowledged her role in saving my life.

That meant more to me than the last deal I closed or building I bought because it made me feel like I was giving back a different way. As I mentioned earlier, one of the key tenets in my life has been *just get it done.* So if I had to put an epitaph on my gravestone, it would be this:

Is it done yet?

Not just done, of course, but done well. I think of all the people who've helped me through the various ordeals I've been through, as well as those who were always there between those and after them.

The doctors and nurses at St. Francis Hospital who helped save my foot . . .

Dr. Herb Lapor and his staff who helped me through my battle with prostate cancer . . .

My son Donald and my brother Laurence who left no stone unturned in facilitating my rescue at sea . . .

My wife Deirdre who has made a better man and enriched my life at every turn and my other children: Devon, Patrick, and Tim.

All of them make me want to do for others what they did for me in my most trying times of greatest needs. The size of a person's wallet means nothing to me compared to the size of their heart. Sure, some of those who were part of our fishing group on the trip to the Abaco Island the Bay Lodge never could have afforded the trip on their own, and the trip was made all the better by their presence, because their company and friendship are priceless to me. The things we value the most in life, the things that are most important, don't need to come with a hefty price tag. Being a good husband, being a good father, being a good grandfather, being a good friend, being someone, people can rely on in their time of need—that's the best recipe for happiness there is.

Sometimes the glass of a fishbowl can make objects inside seem bigger than they are, but that doesn't change their actual size. The same holds true with people and too many of us see exaggerated versions of ourselves from outside the bowl, bigger than life because that's the way so many of us want to view. Yet what matters isn't so much how other people see us as how we see ourselves.

My fishbowl continues to expand, as I search for new ways to use the God Is Good Fund to help others in their struggles as so many have helped me. Indeed, nothing is more personally productive than making a habit out of doing good deeds, simple acts of kindness, no matter how small, every day. We don't live to see our own obituaries, but live your life as if you're writing yours on the go, keeping track of what you want to achieve and what success looks like to you.

I think about my life encapsulated in that long night stranded at sea when I thought I was going to die. It's easier to navigate through channel markers, cans, and nuns than it is to move through life. It's simple to push down the throttle, pass the bell buoys clanging in the gusting wind. It's fun to watch the flocks of terns and gulls dive bombing the water's surface and picking off silversides, mullet, and menhaden. It's easy to leave everything behind in the wake of white water and be free, easy to make a hard bargain with the calm sea. The hard bargain you make with rougher waters is altogether different because you're at their mercy, not able to exert the control that defines you. Yet in relinquishing that control you find yourself a blank slate, free to make yourself into anything you want by embracing the same realities I've come to accept as life lessons:

1. The older you are, the faster time goes by.
2. Life threatening experiences add physical and emotional depth to one's soul if you embrace it.

3. The legacy you leave is the legacy you create.
4. God is good and people are good too.
5. Dare to be different; chart your own path.
6. We look to the past when we want to explain or to justify, and we look to the future to control what is coming our way.
7. All of that time and attention moves us away from the present.
8. The past is over. Embrace what is going on today. Remove distractions.
9. Because in the technically-oriented world, there are plenty of ways to tune out the here and the now.

The journey that we're on weaves and winds along a road whose ends are merely the trappings of new beginnings. It's not the destination that matters anyway, but the journey itself. I learned that the hard way and I hope that, after accompanying me on my own wild ride, you will find yourself on an easier path to happiness, enrichment, fulfillment, friendship, and love.

That's how you can win the hard bargain you've made with life, too.

AFTERWORD

The following was penned by Regina Brett, legendary newspaper writer for the *Plain Dealer* in Cleveland, Ohio, and *New York Times* bestselling author, encapsulating what she calls her "Life Lessons." It is reprinted here with Regina's permission.

The day before I turned 45, I wrote a column of the 45 Lessons Life Taught Me. I added five more lessons when I turned 50. The lessons reflect what I learned from life as a single parent for 18 years, struggling to find the right partner in life, battling breast cancer and healing the bruises from a bumpy childhood. And they reflect what I've learned from readers in my 30 years as a journalist. My Life Lessons ended up e-mailed around the world. It is the most requested column I've ever written.

1. *Life isn't fair, but it's still good.*
2. *When in doubt, just take the next small step.*
3. *Life is too short—enjoy it.*
4. *Your job won't take care of you when you are sick. Your friends and family will.*

5. *Pay off your credit cards every month.*
6. *You don't have to win every argument. Stay true to yourself.*
7. *Cry with someone. It's more healing than crying alone.*
8. *Save for retirement starting with your first pay check.*
9. *When it comes to chocolate, resistance is futile.*
10. *Make peace with your past so it won't screw up the present.*
11. *It's OK to let your children see you cry.*
12. *Don't compare your life to others. You have no idea what their journey is all about.*
13. *If a relationship has to be a secret, you shouldn't be in it . . .*
14. *Take a deep breath. It calms the mind.*
15. *Get rid of anything that isn't useful. Clutter weighs you down in many ways.*
16. *Whatever doesn't kill you really does make you stronger.*
17. *It's never too late to be happy. But it's all up to you and no one else.*
18. *When it comes to going after what you love in life, don't take no for an answer.*
19. *Burn the candles, use the nice sheets, wear the fancy lingerie. Don't save it for a special occasion. Today is special.*
20. *Over prepare, then go with the flow.*
21. *Be eccentric now. Don't wait for old age to wear purple.*
22. *The most important sex organ is the brain.*
23. *No one is in charge of your happiness but you.*
24. *Frame every so-called disaster with these words "In five years, will this matter?"*
25. *Always choose life.*
26. *Forgive but don't forget.*
27. *What other people think of you is none of your business.*
28. *Time heals almost everything. Give time time.*
29. *However good or bad a situation is, it will change.*
30. *Don't take yourself so seriously. No one else does.*
31. *Believe in miracles.*

32. *Don't audit life. Show up and make the most of it now.*
33. *Growing old beats the alternative—dying young.*
34. *Your children get only one childhood.*
35. *All that truly matters in the end is that you loved.*
36. *Get outside every day. Miracles are waiting everywhere.*
37. *If we all threw our problems in a pile and saw everyone else's, we'd grab ours back.*
38. *Envy is a waste of time. Accept what you already have, not what you need.*
39. *The best is yet to come . . .*
40. *No matter how you feel, get up, dress up, and show up.*
41. *Yield.*
42. *All that truly matters in the end is that you loved.*
43. *Envy is a waste of time. You already have all you need.*
44. *If you don't ask, you don't get.*
45. *Life isn't tied with a bow, but it's still a gift.*

I couldn't agree more with all of them, but especially the last one.

Because life really is a gift.

AUTHOR'S NOTE

This book has gone through several versions. One back in 2012, then another in 2019, and they failed to capture my vision for the story. Then I found Jon Land who, right from the start, understood my vision could be best realized by telling the story in three acts, each themed around one of the crises that came to define me.

It was Jon who understood the notion of making a hard bargain with life and living to tell about it. He was also perfect because he's never fished in his life and isn't a waterman. So, unlike the original writers I worked with who were fishermen and outdoorsmen, he was able to focus on the greater story and make it understandable for those who'd never set foot on a boat in their lives. I knew all along the book was about much more than that, and he finally articulated the vision I always had in mind but had never fully verbalized. While the pages we started from formed the building blocks, it was left to us in this version to do the extensive finish work. This book is the product of our hours of deep, thoughtful conversations aimed at bringing that vision to fruition.

Writing a book is a hard bargain in itself because of the strain of bearing one's soul for all to see. But I found it to be well worth the effort for the therapeutic effect it produced. Writing this book helped me reevaluate the experiences that live in my past, as well as provide me with a new perspective to regard the experiences that are unfolding now and are to come. Almost like an emotional reboot that helped me deal with the effects of Post-Traumatic Stress Disorder that have haunted me since my hunting accident and became more severe after I nearly lost my life at sea. So, I wrote this book because I wanted to share my journey to make yours easier.

Beyond that, in writing this book it struck me of how much I have to be grateful for. The worst thing we can do is take for granted the things—health, family, love, friendship—from which true pleasure derives. In that respect, you can look at *Hard Bargain* as a cautionary tale meant to help you keep track of what really matters in life.

You joined me on the wild ride that has been *my* life. Now I invite you to use your gifts to help others and help yourself in the process. To look at life not as a solo act, but as part of a cast that can enrich you as you enrich them. In the course of that ride, I learned God is good and named my fund after that simple principle.

As we close these pages, I invite you to do the same, to embrace our common humanity so the answer to the question, *What did you do today?* becomes, *I helped someone else* because simple acts of kindness are contagious.

A Drawing From Gene
Depicting His Ordeal at Sea

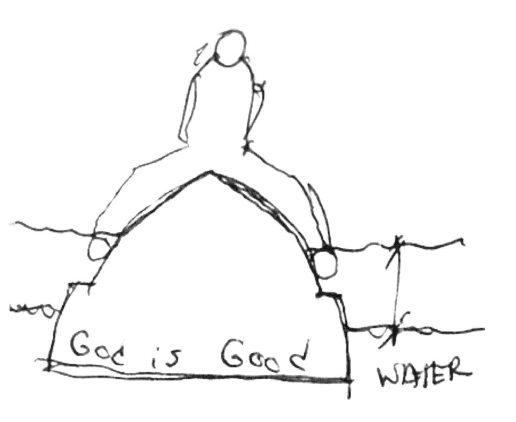

Notes to Myself on My Father's Death

9:30 pm
1/27/86

As I sit here And write this letter
I realize how lucky I Am to have
had the chance to have A Father like Bud
He was one that believed in honesty
loyalty, Sincerely And the true meaning
of forgiveness. He was teaching even when
he didnt realize that he was.
Bud teached many people in many different
ways. ~~~~~~~~~~~~~~~~~ The one thing
I will never forget WAS his Ability to
give people A second chance. Most people
cant understand, infact there were time
I myself had to ~~question~~ his decisions.
But time ~~After~~ And time Again his decisions
were proven to be the right ones ~~~~~~~
~~~~~~~~~~~~~~~~~~~~~~~~~~

   I feel I was extremely lucky in two
respects
   1) "Bud As Dad" - he taught me respect And
the true meaning of it. He taught me how
to love, his way. He was A Father that only
wanted the best for his Family. Family As
far As Bud was concerned didnt stop At
home. As I said before he touched many.
   2) "Dad As Bud" - Not many people have had
the chance to have had their Father As boss
And A good one At that. He taught me to
make intelligent decisions And stick by them.
As he Always used to say to me Donald stick by
the basics when making A decision, And you
~~Bud ~~~~~~~~~~~~~~~~~~~~~~~~~
will Always make the right one

I can remember the days in the hospital
As the were yesterday. Even in the hospital
Bud was conducting business. In fact it wasn't
till close to christmas that Bud began to
speak to the family. And expressed his love to each
member. Bud wasn't one for showing his
emotions but you new they were there thru
his Actions.

I can only sit And wonder why Bud
had to suffer, but I know God had A reason
And that was to pull family the family close.
By doing so, Bud was Able to show his
thru Ability As A Fighter And A good one.

Bud ?????? ??? Re-Assured me that there's
A God out there. While sitting in New
York Hospital one night Bud received 15
Roses Signed From Father Peyton The card
read 15 Roses For 15 Stations of the Rosary
Bud placed the card Away. Two hours late
out of no- where Bud Asked me to give
him the card, While reading the card the
Phone rang Bud said to me that Father Peyton
When I picked up the phone sure enough
it was Father Peyton From Milano

I only hope And play God is As Good
to Bud As Bud was to his family And Friend.
I love you Dad And I will never Forget
you As long As I live, Rest in Peace

Donald

The Homily Father John Denniston
Delivered at My Father's Funeral

29 January 1986

When someone we love suffers and dies many different thoughts, questions, and emotions well up within us. Bud suffered. It seemed so undeserved. When you love someone and they suffer, you know what it means to have stood at Calvary. And the Calvary of cancer is a crucifixion.

Even with religious faith, the death of a loved one is a great tension for us. And yet those of us who were with Bud as his end on earth drew near know that he achieved something. For sure, Bud achieved much that is tangible in this life. He gave much of the tangible away to charities, especially to the Church. But in my estimate, it was in his dying that the story of his greatest achievement is to be found. And that is why this morning, Irene and the family want us to share in their peace of mind and their relief that his suffering is over -- that he is at peace.

A few weeks before Christmas, Bud spoke about the fact that he was having a "happy death." For those of you not of the Catholic religion as well as some of us who are, the expression "happy death" sounds archaic if not implausible. A "happy death" means that we are able to organize our lives for a final time. We have put together the pieces of our years, we review them, patch up relationships, express our love, ask forgiveness, and then speak in the depths of our spirit to the Creator. From my observations, it doesn't lessen the physical pain, but it seems how our spirit grows. How we grow or move into God. Only SOME people are given the gift of a happy death. Bud experienced it and his family knows it.

Bud's dying is not just a story of undeserved pain and anguish. He spoke to each of his family almost as the patriarchs of the Hebrew faith did. He blessed his children.

One evening shortly before Christmas I was privileged to hear him say these words to one of his sons, and I wrote them down. "You've been watching me these last months, and I've been watching you kid. I want you to know how proud I am of you. How confident I am in you. I love you Laurence. What you have been given use intelligently-- keep the faith -- take care of the poor -- stay close to our Catholic faith because it has given me so much."

Who among us have had a parent speak to us so forthrightly, so wisely, so generously? Who among us has received that kind of gift? Who among us have offered it to a loved one? It seems to me that Bud grew in new awareness, new sensitivity, and abilities of expression precisely as he moved closer to his God.

Of course, there is a lighter side to some of this. People were trained to respond to his ringing bell. God save you if you didn't immediately rush in. Phone calls were made and people summoned to what Bud called his "death bed." The strength of his character never yielded. As Brother Kevin Conway well expressed: Just imagine Bud with the Almighty pulling some of his lines. Can't you envision Bud tugging, if you will on God's sleeve with a few humble suggestions. "I'm just a poor pants presser, but have you ever thought about doing some things differently. Why not try it. Give so and so a second chance." Now that God has him, we his friends should be rather confident that Bud will be having God bless us who remain in the kingdom called earth. Some of us in time may be blessed with our own form of a happy death.

We gather in this church - a church to which and in which Bud came to pray, many evenings he walked from the Expressway to St. Mary's and then on home, we gather with tears, an emptiness, and also hope. Hope that comes from what Jesus of Nazareth revealed. A revelation Bud believed. And the Lord's message was so simple. We belong to this world. We belong to one another as family. But we also belong to God. God's plan for us is not a plan of sickness, pain, sadness and death, but the promise of a new beginning. With God there will always be a new beginning. When we die we will be born into His presence. This is what Jesus taught - this is what He promised - this is what Bud believed - this can be our hope.

Finally, I would like to add one personal note. One of the richest gifts that can be offered in this fragile and often paradoxical world is the confidence that a trusted confidente, a true friend offers. Publicly this morning I want to say "thanks Bud" for helping me, for advising me, for wanting me to be a better man and most of all a better priest. May you rest in peace Ben and because of you I will never be ashamed to say: Praised be the name of Jesus Christ.

The kind of duck blind where I suffered my shooting accident.

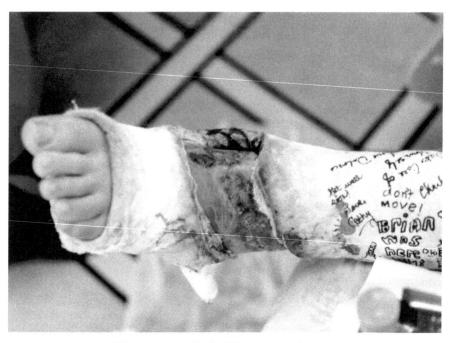

What my injury looked like as it was healing.

*My mother preparing to change
the dressing on my wound.*

*My mother irrigating my wound
before applying a fresh dressing.*

Me, with cane, ready for my junior prom.

Me with my grandmother (aka "Nana").

Me driving my father (passenger seat which is left-side),
Father John, and my friend Jorge to church on a family
vacation to Barbados, my father's favorite place in the world
he called "the closest thing to heaven."

Spending quality time with my father in our den that was used
as a hospital room by both of us.

The rescue pilot's view as he began his search.

Us, amid a vast empty sea, as seen after the pilot had landed his seaplane.

Me pulling the skiff to the plane. Notice Gene's left hand holding onto my extra set of pants attached to the bow eye of the skiff, his literal lifeline that kept him afloat.

Gene being tossed a line to help secure the skiff to the seaplane.

Me holding on to the pontoon of the seaplane,
relieved that our long ordeal was over at last.

Me, Alfred and Gene (left to right) at Marsh Harbour Airport.
Land never felt so good.

The God is Good
—— CHARITABLE FUND ——

As you've just read, nearly losing my life in a boating accident in 2012 left me wanting to save others who were drowning in life, just as I nearly drowned at sea. So I established the **God Is Good Charitable Fund**, dedicated to helping people who have nowhere else to turn. People who, like me on that fateful night stranded at sea, desperately need a helping hand.

The God Is Good Fund extends that hand down to lift them back up at the grassroots level, the basis for what one of the inaugural recipients, the Troy family, said was "absolutely a miracle." I don't call it a miracle; I call it an obligation. I stepped in to rescue the Troys by rebuilding their home after Superstorm Sandy, just as I had been rescued at sea.

There have been many storms since and many more to come, both figurative and literal. And toward that end, the God Is Good Fund has supported high schools, colleges, pre-schools, inner city education, and places of worship. The fund has also contributed to the causes of law enforcement, firefighters, and the Coast Guard, including widows and orphans left behind by tragedy, as well as community health and mental health and well-being issues.

And here's the good news: You don't need to have a life-changing experience to want to change lives. You don't have to suffer to make a difference in the lives of others who are suffering. You can join me and others who've already made an impact by supporting the God Is Good Fund here:

www.thegodisgoodcharitablefund.com

No cause is too small or too large for the God Is Good Fund to champion, because heartache and misery can afflict anyone at any time. Almost perishing that night at sea taught me that you can't really put a dollar sign on love, or happiness, or family, or friendship, or loyalty, but all of them are worth more than anything that comes with a price tag.

"If not us, who? If not now, when?" President John F. Kennedy once asked.

And that is exactly what the God Is Good Fund is all about.

Printed in the USA
CPSIA information can be obtained
at www.ICGtesting.com
JSHW070303160424
61198JS00007B/19

9 781963 296358